AUDIT COMMITTEE EFFECTIVENESS — WHAT WORKS BEST
2nd Edition

Prepared by

Principal Authors
Richard M. Steinberg, *Project Leader*
Catherine L. Bromilow, *Project Manager*

Project Sponsor
John W. Copley

Sponsored by
The Institute of Internal Auditors Research Foundation

ISBN 0-89413-446-9
00192 11/00
First Printing

CONTENTS

ABOUT THE AUTHORS

Richard M. Steinberg

Rick Steinberg is a senior partner of PricewaterhouseCoopers LLP and its Professional, Technical, Risk & Quality Leader for Corporate Governance, responsible for design and development of PwC's corporate governance program, thought leadership, and serving major companies on governance and related issues.

Mr. Steinberg is a founder of his firm's risk management and control consulting practice and served as its global leader, overseeing development of client service capabilities around the world and serving as senior resource on international engagements. In addition to leading this study, *Audit Committee Effectiveness — What Works Best, 2nd Edition,* he led development of the companion report, *Corporate Governance and the Board — What Works Best.* He served as lead project partner on the team that developed the landmark study, *Internal Control — Integrated Framework*, published by the Committee of Sponsoring Organizations of the Treadway Commission (COSO) and which has gained recognition as *the* standard of internal control. He also spearheaded development of PwC's interactive system providing leading-edge industry, best practice and benchmarking information to PwC's client service professionals worldwide.

Mr. Steinberg has long been a leader in shaping professional standards, serving as chair, co-chair or member of many committees and task forces of the American Institute of CPAs. He is a member of the Conference Board's Global Corporate Governance Research Center Advisory Board, and was selected by COSO to serve on its Advisory Council for developing guidance on specialized business issues. He is widely published, authoring books, monographs and articles in leading journals, and is a sought-after speaker by business, professional and academic organizations. He is a graduate of the University of Pennsylvania's Wharton School, holds an MBA from New York University's Graduate School of Business, and is recognized in *Who's Who in Finance and Industry*.

Catherine L. Bromilow

Catherine Bromilow is a senior manager with the Corporate Governance Services group of PricewaterhouseCoopers LLP. She works with boards of directors of major companies and institutions bringing best practice and enhancing programs to comply with evolving regulations and expectations. Most recently she has worked with audit committees, benchmarking processes and performance against both best practice and the new regulatory and exchange listing rules, based on Blue Ribbon Committee recommendations.

Ms. Bromilow was the project manager for this study, *Audit Committee Effectiveness — What Works Best, 2nd Edition,* and its companion report, *Corporate Governance and the Board — What Works Best.* She has had management responsibility on audit and consulting engagements in the United States and Canada, and was selected for secondment to the Canada Deposit Insurance Corporation. Previously, she served as internal audit manager at the Toronto-Dominion Bank, assisting the bank to achieve its risk management, corporate governance and regulatory compliance objectives.

Ms. Bromilow speaks at international conferences and seminars on corporate governance, compliance, ethics and risk management, and has lectured at the university level. She is a Chartered Accountant from Canada and holds both Master of Accounting and BA (Honours Chartered Accountancy Studies) degrees from the University of Waterloo.

ABOUT THE TEAM

This book is sponsored and published as a part of The IIA Research Foundation's Master Key series. The IIA (www.theiia.org) is the internal auditing profession's acknowledged leader, recognized authority, and chief educator. The Foundation mirrors The IIA's leadership by providing internal auditing practitioners, executive management, and corporate governance entities with valuable materials, such as this book and its counterpart, *Corporate Governance and the Board — What Works Best.*

PricewaterhouseCoopers is proud of our collaboration with The IIA Research Foundation and our authorship of this study, *Audit Committee Effectiveness — What Works Best, 2nd Edition.* PricewaterhouseCoopers (www.pwcglobal.com) is the world's largest professional services organization. Drawing on the knowledge and skills of more than 150,000 people in 150 countries, we help our clients solve complex business problems and measurably enhance their ability to build value, manage risk, and improve performance in an Internet-enabled world. PricewaterhouseCoopers refers to the member firms of the worldwide PricewaterhouseCoopers organization.

Advisory Team
Charles H. Allen
LeRoy E. Bookal, CIA
Stephen A. Doherty
Gareth Evans
Jane F. Mutchler
Claire Beth Nilsen

The Institute of Internal Auditors
Headquarters Staff
William G. Bishop III, CIA,
President, The Institute of Internal Auditors
Basil H. Pflumm, CIA, *Vice President, Practices Center;*
Executive Director, The IIA Research Foundation
Eugene J. O'Neill, CIA, *Director of Finance and Customer Services*
Susan B. Lione, CIA, CCSA, *Senior Manager, Research*
Trish W. Harris, *Senior Manager, Corporate Marketing,*
Media Relations and Public Relations
Wendy Acha, *Research Administrator*
Nicki Creatore, *Research Administrator*

ABOUT THIS REPORT

With increasing attention to financial reporting—by regulators, security analysts, institutional investors and others—the corporate financial reporting process and the audit committee's role in it are under intense scrutiny. Much of the focus is on committee members' qualifications, their independence from management, information they receive from auditors, and what committees report publicly to the company's shareholders.

At the same time, boards of directors are delegating increasing responsibilities to the audit committee. In addition to oversight of the financial reporting process, more audit committees are monitoring compliance with laws and regulations and the company's code of conduct, and over-seeing risk management and a broader range of internal control. As more and more is asked of the audit committee, its members work harder to keep up.

First published in 1993, this guide provides direction to audit committee members on how best to carry out their responsibilities. It has been updated, revamped and expanded to address the many new rules and emerging best practices. It is global in scope, based on practices of companies with well-developed corporate governance processes, rules of countries with advanced regulatory structures, and recommendations of leading professional and other bodies. It was developed with face-to-face input from some of the most experienced, knowledgeable audit committee members around, as well as ideas of thought leaders, surveys of audit committee and other board members, and PricewaterhouseCoopers' own experience with leading companies and their boards and audit committees.

This guide is designed to help you and your audit committee colleagues deal with not only your existing responsibilities based on current rules and expectations, but also emerging forces driving those expectations and where they will lead audit committees going forward.

You might have seen *Corporate Governance and the Board — What Works Best*, providing leading-edge guidance on the broader responsibilities of the full board of directors. That ground-breaking publication, to which this is the companion document, has been extremely well received by the director community and is being looked to by many boards as their guiding benchmark. We hope you find this book as useful.

PricewaterhouseCoopers LLP

HOW TO USE IT

With directors among the most time-pressured executives, this report is organized to let you go directly to areas of greatest interest.

The first two chapters discuss the audit committee's major responsibilities and how they are most effectively carried out. The next five cover relationships, resources, meetings and other activities that, done well, enable the committee to be effective in meeting its core responsibilities.

The last chapter looks to the future—to where today's emerging forces will take the audit committee in the coming years.

What's in the Chapter

Financial Statements

Fundamental to success is the financial reporting process. This chapter focuses on what you need to do in reviewing the financial statements, including what to look for in high-risk judgment areas, new accounting treatments and changes in the financial reports. Also highlighted is interim financial reporting, and why and how the committee should pay attention.

Risk, Control, Compliance

Today, most audit committees' responsibility extends well beyond financial reporting and related internal control, encompassing overseeing processes for monitoring compliance with laws, regulations and the corporate code of conduct, conducting special investigations and other matters. This chapter explains what's expected, and why it's crucial that there be clear understanding with the full board as to where the committee's scope ends and the full board's begins.

Interaction with Management, Auditors

Strength and candor of the audit committee's working relationships with management and the auditors determine the committee's success. You will see how the committee can best interact with key management personnel, the internal audit director and external auditors, what to expect from each, and where to probe.

Committee Composition

Having the right directors on the committee—with the right mix of knowledge, judgment, independence and commitment—is key to success. This chapter takes you through the new member selection process, independence requirements and issues like committee size and length of members' service terms.

Training and Resources

Attributes making an effective audit committee member—integrity, diligence, inquisitiveness and sound judgment—are intrinsic qualities, but others like knowledge of financial reporting and company financial systems aren't. You'll be advised of what you need to know, including orientations for new committee members and ongoing training for others, and what additional resources support committee success.

Charter, Evaluation, Reporting

In this chapter you'll be apprised of what the committee charter needs to cover, based on best practice and new rules. Also highlighted are how committees evaluate themselves against various benchmarks, and what the committee needs to report to the board, shareholders and others.

Meetings

This topic might seem mundane, but how often committee meetings are held and for how long, who is invited and what type of advance materials are provided all are critical. This chapter covers those matters, as well as which topics to cover when, and with whom, and when to hold private meetings.

The Future

Do you want to peer into our crystal ball? You'll see how past events and new forces emerging today will shape audit committees and their activities going forward.

How Is Our Audit Committee Doing?

A self-assessment guide allows you quickly to see how well your committee stacks up against these leading practices. Also provided for your consideration are an audit committee charter and discussion of a topic many audit committee members are looking to better understand—e-business.

CHAPTER 1
FINANCIAL STATEMENTS

The activities of the audit committee vary depending on company circumstances and needs of its board of directors. Generally, audit committees have responsibility for overseeing:

- Reliability of financial reporting
- Effectiveness of internal control over financial reporting
- Process for monitoring compliance with regulatory matters
- Process for monitoring compliance with the corporate code of conduct

Increasingly, audit committees are taking on additional oversight responsibilities, including broad-based risk management and control, and conducting special investigations, among others. A committee that clearly understands its key responsibilities as delegated from the full board, and the best ways to carry them out, is positioned to discharge those responsibilities effectively.

The committee's responsibilities for reviewing the financial statements are addressed here, with its other responsibilities discussed in Chapter 2.

Annual Financial Reporting

The audit committee's most important role is overseeing the financial reporting process. A key element is reviewing and discussing the annual financial statements and determining whether they are complete, and consistent with operational and other information known to committee members. But the committee's financial reporting responsibilities don't end there. The committee also needs to:

- Understand and be comfortable with the information systems and processes used in developing the financial statements
- Review significant accounting and reporting issues, including recent professional and regulatory pronouncements, and understand their impact on the financial statements
- Ask management and the internal and external auditors about significant risks and exposures and plans to minimize the risks
- Meet with management and the external auditors to review the financial statements and results of the audit
- Consider management's handling of proposed audit adjustments identified by the external auditors

How can committee members best do this? By thorough preparation before meetings—carefully considering the draft financial statements and other information provided—and frank discussions with management and the auditors.

In conducting these activities, the audit committee needs to focus on specific issues, including accounting principles, judgment areas, significant changes and narrative reporting.

Accounting Principles

Audit committees must understand the significant accounting principles followed by the company and assess whether they are reasonable and appropriate in the circumstances. They should look to management and the external auditors to identify changes in accounting principles adopted by the company. Two types of changes can occur—those mandated by new accounting or regulatory rules and those made at management's discretion.

The committee should be sure its members are briefed on changes in accounting and reporting standards, in time to consider new rules when reviewing the financial statements. A discussion might be led by management or the external auditors, or both, covering:

- What new standards will affect the company for the first time this present year
- What new standards will affect the company for the first time in a future year
- How standards under development, when adopted, might affect the company's financial statements

Management may elect to change accounting principles for a number of reasons: a change in how the company conducts its business, a particular matter becoming more significant, or to conform with prevalent industry practice. Some companies, however, seek change to mask deteriorating earnings or meet earnings targets. The committee should carefully question management's rationale for any discretionary changes. Questions to consider include:

- Why is the change being proposed?
- What is the effect on income for the current and future periods?
- What effect will the change have on the company's loan covenants?
- What effect will it have on executive compensation or bonus plans?
- What method do our principal competitors follow?
- If this is a change to adopt a "preferable" method, why was it not proposed in previous years?
- What effect, if any, will the change have on relations with our institutional investors?
- Will regulators object to the change?
- What is the effect of not implementing the change?
- What do the external auditors think of the change?

Public companies' financial statements and their underlying accounting principles are subject to external scrutiny—from analysts, regulators, investors and the media. The audit committee should ask whether criticisms of the company's accounting policies have surfaced, understand their source and nature, and discuss them with management and the external auditors. There have been well-publicized instances of companies that ignored such criticisms, or otherwise used undesirable accounting, and subsequently were required to restate their financial results, with related adverse investor and market reaction, public embarrassment and even legal action.

Areas Involving Judgment

Judgmental areas such as those involving valuation of assets and liabilities can significantly affect a company's reported profits and should be scrutinized by the audit committee. Judgments are commonly required for:

- Likely uncollectible accounts receivable
- Slow-moving or obsolete inventory
- Asset impairments
- Pension and other postretirement benefit obligations
- Restructuring costs
- Loan losses
- Derivatives
- Future warranty, product and environmental liabilities
- Litigation reserves
- Other commitments and contingencies
- Transactions structured specifically to achieve certain accounting results

Reality is that for many of these estimates management must predict the effects of events that might not occur until long into the future. While many companies have well-established methods of handling relatively routine estimates, others can prove more difficult. On the positive side, most audit committees request timely information on the degree to which significant litigation and claims, tax liabilities and other estimates are reflected in the financial statements. Looking back to our 1993 survey, we found that about 85 percent of audit committees discussed significant accruals and reserves, and recent experience shows this area continues to receive audit committee attention. On the other hand, some audit committee members don't fully recognize the extent to which improper "managing" of reported earnings often is accomplished via manipulation of estimates and reserves, and fail to give this area enough attention.

While recognizing that estimates by their nature are subjective and subject to change based on future events and honest differences of opinion, knowledgeable audit committee members recognize estimates' susceptibility to manipulation and give them the necessary scrutiny.

In considering estimates, these audit committees make sure they:

- Consider the quality of systems and reliability of data underlying the estimates
- Understand key business assumptions and dependencies supporting estimates
- Understand why management did or did not record a particular estimate or reserve
- Understand the reasons underlying the timing and amounts of accruals, such as restructuring provisions and asset write-downs
- Monitor increases in and charges against significant reserves established in prior periods
- Inquire of management whether the reserve balances continue to be appropriate

With this information, and applying its knowledge of the company's business performance, the committee can then make informed decisions on the acceptability of estimates to be reflected in the financial statements.

Significant Changes

Best practice calls for the audit committee to review significant period-to-period changes in the accounts as an integral part of the financial statement review. Management should explain the reasons for major variations from year to year and between actual results and budgets or forecasts. Additionally, it is useful for the committee to understand whether the final quarter's results divert significantly from the trend witnessed in the first three quarters and, if so, why. Importantly, the committee should ask management to address why significant variances did not occur when business circumstances indicate they should have.

Any unusual or complex items and their accounting treatment should be highlighted for the committee. As noted, particular attention should be paid to management's reasoning in areas requiring the exercise of significant judgment or estimates. Highly complex issues, such as derivatives, should be explained and discussed. Committee members should be satisfied that explanations supplied by management are reasonable and consistent with their understanding of the company.

Narrative Reporting

Public companies in a number of countries are required to provide additional disclosure of the companies' risks and results, such as management's discussion and analysis in the United States. In other countries it may be referred to as management commentary or yearly review. Whatever form the reporting takes, the audit committee should review it and other sections of the annual report before publication and consider whether the company is disclosing enough information and that it is consistent with the financial statements and facts as the committee understands them. Committee members also should inquire whether the disclosures comply with regulatory requirements.

The committee also may inquire of the external auditors and the internal audit director whether the narrative reporting information is adequate and consistent with the financial statements and their knowledge of the company's operations.

Exhibit 1.1 outlines our 1999 survey results on audit committee oversight of financial reporting.

Exhibit 1.1: Audit Committees and Annual Financial Reports

Audit committees that:

- Review and approve year-end earnings **before** they are released — 91%

- Oversee the processes to identify and control the risks in producing financial information — 88%

- Determine whether initial selection of a significant accounting principle (or a change) is consistent with underlying business practices — 82%

- Consult with management and the external auditors and approve initial selection of a significant accounting principle (or a change) before financial statements are released — 82%

Source: Audit Committee Chair Survey

Interim Financial Statements

Interim reports have become increasingly important to investors and security analysts. With lower-than-expected reported interim earnings driving down stock price, management often is under significant pressure to report numbers that meet the "Street's" expectations. That pressure, coupled with the typical circumstance where processes surrounding interim reporting are less rigorous than for annual reporting, increases the possibility of a company issuing misstated interim results.

Given the importance of interim earnings, every audit committee should consider whether it is sufficiently involved in overseeing the reporting process. Timely audit committee review of interim results has many benefits, including:

- Allowing the committee to identify and direct attention to significant issues on a proactive basis, enhancing its understanding of the company's business
- Facilitating management's providing to the committee relevant financial information on a timely basis, assisting the year-end review process and enhancing lines of communication between management and the committee
- Enhancing communication between the auditors and the committee
- Ultimately strengthening the financial reporting process

Regulatory and other influential bodies around the world, including the Blue Ribbon Committee (BRC) on Improving the Effectiveness of Corporate Audit Committees, have recognized the benefits to be gained with increased audit committee involvement in overseeing interim earnings. And, in 1999, with the Securities and Exchange Commission's (SEC) rule implementing the BRC recommendation, already practiced by the largest accounting firms, that external auditors review interim financial information before filing, we expect to see audit committees of companies in the United States take a more active role in reviewing interim results.

In its review, the committee should inquire of management about significant judgments and issues faced in closing the books, and whether the interim statements were prepared on a basis consistent with the annual financial statements. It should discuss with management the overall quality of earnings and adequacy of disclosures to be made. Many questions posed during the annual report review—how results compare with budget, whether accounting principles are consistently applied, how unusual events are reflected, etc.—apply to interim reports.

Where the external auditors review interim financial statements, the audit committee should expect to receive relevant information. The American Institute of Certified Public Accountants requires external auditors to communicate specified matters. These include uncorrected probable material misstatements due to departures from generally accepted accounting principles, material accounting or disclosure matters identified as not correct, and issues like those that need to be reported to the committee in connection with audits of the annual financial statements (discussed in Chapter 3). Such communication is preferably accomplished before the interim reports are filed with regulators.

Although it's best when the audit committee meets in person to discuss interim results with management and the external auditors, some committees find it satisfactory instead to hold a conference call, or for the committee chair to speak with management and the auditors, and then report back to the full committee.

Other Critical Disclosures

While disclosures of annual and interim financial results are fundamental elements of corporate reporting, management communicates a great deal of other information—both financial and non-financial—to various stakeholders. Concern over the fairness of such disclosures has prompted regulators to issue or consider rules aimed at eliminating "selective disclosure," thereby leveling the playing field for all investors. The lead was taken in the United States when the SEC in 2000 issued Regulation Fair Disclosure, requiring a company disclosing material nonpublic information to securities market professionals and securities holders to make such disclosures public—either simultaneously for an intentional disclosure or promptly for an unintentional one. Audit committees charged with monitoring the fairness of corporate communications on behalf of the board should understand the applicable rules and how management ensures compliance. Further discussion of disclosure practices and the board's role can be found in Chapter 7, "Telling the World," in the companion report, *Corporate Governance and the Board — What Works Best.*

CHAPTER 2
RISK, CONTROL, COMPLIANCE

In addition to reviewing the company's financial statements, most audit committees have responsibility for overseeing the financial reporting process, monitoring compliance with laws and regulations and the corporate code of conduct, and conducting special investigations. This chapter addresses these and other committee activities.

Risk and Internal Control

Companies face numerous risks emanating from the nature of their operations, the economic environment in which they operate and other sources. Internal factors, such as the control environment and quality of accounting processes, and external factors, like the economy's strength and regulatory changes, present risks that affect financial reports. It is these risks—that the company's financial statements might be materially misstated, either intentionally or unintentionally—on which audit committees historically have focused. Well-designed and implemented internal control reduces the risk of financial statements being materially misstated. Since the Foreign Corrupt Practices Act (FCPA) was passed in 1977, publicly held companies in the United States have recognized an increased responsibility for internal control. The audit committee should be aware that the FCPA requires public companies, among other things, to keep reasonably detailed records of all transactions and to maintain internal accounting controls providing reasonable assurance that the transactions are properly authorized and recorded.

The landmark COSO report, *Internal Control — Integrated Framework*, issued in 1992, defines internal control much more broadly than those controls related to reliable financial reporting. It defines internal control as a process that provides reasonable assurance that a company will be able to achieve its objectives in the following areas:

- Effectiveness and efficiency of operations
- Reliability of financial reporting
- Compliance with applicable laws and regulations

The controls that help ensure the quality of the key financial reports are clearly within the audit committee's scope. But companies' internal control systems have broader objectives relating to achieving their fundamental business goals, as well as legal and regulatory compliance. Some committees limit their focus to the financial reporting controls, whereas others also oversee the controls that ensure legal and regulatory compliance, and still others oversee all three areas of internal control. While the scope of internal control oversight may vary from company to company, it is critical that there be a clear understanding between the full board and audit committee as to the extent of the audit committee's responsibility.

A fuller discussion of risk management and the board's role is contained in the companion document to this report, *Corporate Governance and the Board — What Works Best*.

Once the audit committee has agreed with the board on the scope of its oversight of internal control, how can it get information on the state of control? Management should identify the major risks, assess their potential impact and take appropriate actions to mitigate key risks.

The committee should review with management its assessment and whether the risk factors are being reasonably addressed. In addition, the committee may wish to seek independent assurance from a more objective source, including internal and external auditors.

The 2000 report of the American Institute of Certified Public Accountants (AICPA) Public Oversight Board (POB) Panel on Audit Effectiveness includes the recommendation that audit committees increase the time and attention they devote to discussions of internal control with management and the internal and external auditors. Specifically, the report recommends that committees obtain written reports from management on the effectiveness of internal control over financial reporting and that specific expectations be established with management and the auditors on qualitative internal control information needs of the committee. Such qualitative information should include views on the control environment and controls over financial reporting.

Why does management need to be front and center in these discussions? Because management has primary responsibility for control—for setting the tone at the top, for establishing controls and for ensuring they are effectively carried out.

Both the internal and external auditors assess internal control in the course of their audits, but typically from different perspectives. It's important that the committee understand the extent of the assessment of controls, so it does not place assurance inappropriately on auditors' work.

The Institute of Internal Auditors *Standards for the Professional Practice of Internal Auditing (Standards)*, issued initially in 1978, are under revision. The August 2000 draft revised *Standards* direct internal auditors to evaluate internal controls regarding the:

- Information systems environment
- Reliability and integrity of financial and operational information
- Effectiveness and efficiency of operations
- Safeguarding of assets
- Compliance with laws, regulations and contracts

In any particular year, the internal audit plan may call for some or all of these types of controls to be covered by testing.

The external auditors, on the other hand, are required to test internal controls only over areas where they intend to rely on particular controls in the financial statement audit. To the extent the external auditors do not rely on the internal control system, but rather obtain audit satisfaction through substantive tests of year-end balances, they normally do not test the related controls.

Because of differences in responsibilities, audit approaches and scope, the audit committee should understand the extent to which each auditor's work can be expected to detect internal control weaknesses or fraud. As well as understanding the work performed, the committee should review with both the internal and external auditors their identification of internal control weaknesses.

Throughout the year, internal auditing typically issues many reports to different business units and departments, containing assessments and comments on internal control. The audit committee rarely receives each report, and normally doesn't need to. Instead, internal audit prepares periodic reports for the committee, identifying units audited and summarizing the most significant issues. Significant audit findings may include misstatements, illegal acts, errors, inefficiency, ineffectiveness, conflicts of interest and control weaknesses.

The external auditors also will see that significant control deficiencies identified in the course of audit work are reported to the committee.

Having received reports of the respective auditors, the audit committee should ask management its plans for addressing these matters. Management is responsible for weighing the consequences of a control weakness versus the cost of implementing corrective action. Management should inform the committee whether, as a result of its cost/benefit analysis, it intends to act on the recommendations. The audit committee needs to critically assess the adequacy of management's response, particularly in cases where management has rejected a recommendation to correct a significant control deficiency.

It's also important for the committee to monitor the timeliness of management's corrective action. While management may agree with the finding and the action needed, delays in correcting issues expose the company to ongoing risk. The audit committee should obtain progress reports from management or the auditors.

E-Business

E-business is changing the way companies do business, and the related risks and internal controls are of increasing importance to audit committees. Committee members need to understand the implications and, for those risks falling within the committee's purview, be comfortable that management has satisfactorily addressed them. Because of the rapidly expanding relevance of e-business, these issues are discussed more fully in Appendix C to this report.

External Reporting on Control

While internal communications about internal control are commonplace, reporting to external parties is not. And where reporting on internal control does exist, its nature varies significantly.

In the United Kingdom, since 1995, the Cadbury Code requires directors to describe the system of internal financial controls and state that they have reviewed its effectiveness. In 1998, the Hampel Committee's *Combined Code* recommended that "the directors should, at least annually, conduct a review of the effectiveness of the group's system of internal control and should report to shareholders that they have done so. The review should cover all controls, including financial, operational and compliance controls and risk management." The precise format for the directors' report was not prescribed, but to provide added guidance, the Turnbull Committee was established and in 1999 issued *Internal Control: Guidance for Directors on the Combined Code.* Companies listed in the United Kingdom are required to make a statement of compliance with the *Combined Code* in their annual report, with full compliance, including the disclosure requirements, required for many companies in 2000.

In the United States the debate has focused on positive reporting, that is, public reporting on the adequacy, or effectiveness, of internal control, although reporting continues to be limited. In 1987 the Treadway Commission recommended that the Securities and Exchange Commission (SEC) require management to report to shareholders on the effectiveness of internal control. The SEC proposed such reporting, but never required it. The POB of the AICPA in a 1993 report also supported public reporting on internal control over financial reporting. In one industry, banking, reporting became required when the Federal Deposit Insurance Company Improvement Act mandated that large banks publicly issue internal control reports. The General Accounting Office in its 1996 *Report on the Accounting Profession — Major Issues: Progress and Concerns*, said that SEC support is critical to further progress in internal control reporting, and that, in the long run, such reporting will be expanded either because of market demand or a systemic crisis. Thus far, public reporting on internal control generally has been limited to statements in some companies' annual reports to shareholders on management's responsibility for internal control. The POB Panel on Audit Effectiveness believes this may change, noting in its 2000 report that as the demand for new and timelier information arises, management and auditor reporting on controls may become inevitable.

As to companies that do issue a report or other statement on internal control, the audit committee certainly should look into management's assessment and reporting processes, obtaining information and asking relevant questions necessary to carry out its oversight responsibilities in this area.

Regulatory, Legal and Tax Matters

Companies face increasingly complex environments, as they need to track and comply with all manner of law and regulation. While boards of directors have long focused attention on monitoring compliance issues, their attention to legal and regulatory compliance heightened in 1991 with the issuance in the United States of the Federal Sentencing Guidelines. The Guidelines, which continue to have a significant impact on companies doing business in the United States, whether incorporated there or not, affect penalties when a company is convicted of felonies and certain misdemeanors. They target antitrust violations, bid rigging, securities violations, price fixing, bribery, embezzlement, mail fraud and numerous other criminal activities. Factors that influence the fines are the seriousness of the crime and culpability of the company—but a company's fine can be reduced if mitigating factors exist. One is if a company detects the offense and reports it to the proper authorities, and the second is the existence of an effective internal control program—covering compliance—in place before the crime was committed.

Under the Guidelines, to be considered to have an effective compliance program, a company must meet *minimum* requirements. Specifically, it must:

- Establish compliance standards and procedures reasonably capable of reducing the prospect of criminal conduct
- Assign a specific high-level person to oversee compliance with the standards and procedures
- Use due care not to delegate substantial discretionary authority to individuals whom the company knows or should know have a propensity to engage in illegal activities
- Establish training programs and educational material to communicate the compliance standards and procedures to employees
- Take reasonable steps to achieve compliance with the standards, including continuous monitoring and auditing systems and a reporting system to allow anonymous reporting of suspected criminal conduct
- Consistently enforce the standards with appropriate discipline
- When an offense is detected, respond appropriately and take action to prevent future occurrences

Added impetus to board focus on compliance came in 1994 with the Caremark International, Inc. case, now considered a landmark. Here, the influential Delaware court ruled that a board needs to assure itself that information and reporting systems exist to provide senior management and the board with timely, accurate information allowing them to judge both the company's compliance with laws and its business performance—and that directors have an affirmative duty to determine whether the company has effective compliance programs. Observers note that this represented a major change from the prior level of responsibility, which was to act only if a director suspected illegal activity.

While in some companies legal and regulatory compliance is addressed by the full board, for many, compliance falls within the purview of the audit committee. In our 1999 survey, 82 percent of audit committee chairs said their committee has responsibility for overseeing the program for compliance with laws and regulations, compared with 46 percent in 1993. The National Association of Corporate Directors' 1999–2000 Public Company Governance Survey found that 66 percent of audit committees oversee legal liability, up from 50 percent in 1995.

How can an audit committee that takes on oversight of compliance programs be effective? Actions include:

- Reviewing the effectiveness of the company's system for monitoring compliance with laws and regulations
- Understanding the nature of any significant issues that come to light and management's investigation and follow-up, including disciplinary actions
- Reviewing trends in compliance and management's plans to address systemic issues
- Reviewing findings and reports of examinations by regulators
- Ensuring that management has reflected the impact of significant issues in the financial reports

Periodic briefings and information from the internal audit director, general counsel, compliance officer, external auditors and management provide the committee with much of the information it needs. In particular, internal audit can play an important role if it tests compliance with laws, regulations and the company's related policies. Our 1999 survey shows that 61 percent of internal audit directors provide the audit committee with frequent or occasional written reports on company compliance with key laws and regulations.

Even if another board committee monitors compliance, the audit committee still needs to understand any major compliance issues so that it can consider the financial statement impact.

Codes of Conduct and Ethical Behavior

Many companies establish codes of conduct to formally communicate to all employees guidelines for acceptable business practice. Codes cover a variety of subjects, but consistent themes are honesty, integrity, fairness and legal compliance. Some companies include conflict of interest policies in their codes; others have separate policy statements. Whatever its specific contents, a code plays an important role in setting the "tone at the top" in a company.

Many audit committees oversee codes of conduct and ethical standards on behalf of the full board. Our 1999 survey shows 77 percent of audit committees with responsibility to oversee business ethics monitoring processes. Best practice finds that committees bearing this responsibility:

- Ensure that a robust, written code of conduct has been developed and communicated to all employees
- Review the support and communications channels available to help employees deal with issues
- Review the program for monitoring compliance with the code and summary results it reports
- Ensure that management complies with the code and exhibits ethical behavior, in its vital role in establishing the tone at the top

Management, the general counsel, internal audit director and ethics officer, if one exists, can provide relevant information to the committee on the code's implementation throughout the company. In our 1999 survey, 69 percent of the internal audit directors said they provide the audit committee written reports on compliance with their company's code.

More guidance on considerations when monitoring ethical conduct is found in Chapter 3, "Tone at the Top," in the companion report, *Corporate Governance and the Board — What Works Best.*

Special Investigations

The audit committee charter should empower the committee to conduct any special investigations it deems necessary to meet its responsibilities. The subject of an investigation might involve significant fraud, violation of the code of conduct, or an illegal act. Investigations sometimes involve intentional or unintentional accounting misstatements, such as recording fictitious sales in the belief real sales will catch up in the next period, discovery of side letters to contracts that change the nature of the transactions, and adjustment of reserves with the goal of smoothing earnings. The audit committee chair should be informed of any such matter as soon as possible so that an investigation can be initiated.

Principal resources available to the audit committee include internal audit, general counsel, an independent law firm, and the external auditors or another accounting firm engaged to assist the committee. Selection of resources depends on circumstances. If the situation is restricted to a remote location, corporate management might be involved in the investigation. If, however, there is an allegation of management fraud and collusion, the audit committee may decide to use external parties exclusively and limit the dissemination of information concerning the investigation.

Whomever the audit committee designates to participate, it is important that committee members be kept apprised of progress. It may be necessary to expand or limit the investigation as more facts become known. While it is critical to determine what happened and deal appropriately with the event, the investigation also should focus on how it happened and what steps need to be taken to reduce the likelihood of recurrence of the same or similar situations.

A Word of Caution

The audit committee must undertake many activities just to carry out its core responsibilities effectively. Because often audit committee members understand the company's risk management and control systems better than most directors, there is a tendency by some boards to put increasing responsibility for monitoring other aspects of risk management on the audit committee. The audit committee needs to be careful to keep itself from becoming overburdened by those and other added tasks. With audit committee responsibilities already having expanded, it is becoming more important that any further responsibility transfer be carefully considered, ensuring the committee has sufficient time to successfully address its core financial reporting oversight responsibility.

It is up to the audit committee to judge whether its current scope is appropriate or excessive, and whether it should take on additional duties that the board may wish to assign. Whatever duties the board and audit committee agree upon should be clearly specified in the committee's charter, so all directors understand its scope. This also enables the board to identify where important responsibilities have not yet been assigned, to be sure nothing "falls through the cracks."

CHAPTER 3
INTERACTION WITH
MANAGEMENT, AUDITORS

The strength and candor of the audit committee's working relationships with management and the internal and external auditors are key factors enabling the audit committee to effectively carry out its responsibilities.

Relationship with Management

Successful accomplishment of the audit committee's duties and responsibilities requires significant interaction with management. Management typically takes the lead in presenting to the committee reports on such matters as reviews of operating results and financial statements, significant estimates inherent in the financial statements, adequacy of reserves, financial reporting risk analysis, adequacy of controls, impact of changes in accounting, emerging accounting issues, and so forth. But management's participation in the committee's meetings, while essential, is not enough. Management's ongoing and meaningful dialogue with the committee further contributes to its understanding of the company's business and operations—crucial to the committee's ability to oversee the company's financial reporting. Information the audit committee should obtain through discussions with management and written reports includes:

- Management's assessment of the business risks the company faces, and its planned responses to those risks
- Controls over treasury activities, including cash management, hedging, foreign currency transactions and use of new or unusual financial instruments
- The legal environment, including the status of pending lawsuits or administrative proceedings and related accruals, if any, and the status of product and environmental liability and warranty reserves
- Industry-specific issues, such as regulatory issues or information about the competitive environment
- The effect new tax laws and other regulations may have on the company
- The company's foreign operations, including locations, and controls over financial reporting
- Insurance coverage for directors and officers
- Extent of work performed for governments and compliance with related contractual terms
- The company's policies and procedures for reviewing officers' expenses and perquisites

While management is a principal source of information, the committee, in its independent oversight role, needs to objectively evaluate whether it is receiving the right information and the appropriate level of detail. As discussed below, audit committees look to the internal audit director and external auditors for balance and input in assessing information provided to them.

There are times when the committee should meet privately with members of management. Private meetings are appropriate when, for example, the appointment, reappointment or dismissal of the internal audit director or external auditors is being considered. Audit committee executive meetings, limited to only committee members, are also important, and the vast majority of committees meet in executive session—necessary for candid discussion of management's effectiveness.

Relationship with Internal Auditing

Internal auditing functions are common in large companies, as well as many middle market entities, and are a valuable resource to the audit committee—referred to by one audit committee chair as "the eyes and ears for the audit committee." In fulfilling its oversight role, the audit committee reviews internal audit's activities, organizational structure, qualifications and effectiveness. If there isn't an internal audit function in a company, the audit committee should periodically revisit that decision with management.

One of the most important responsibilities of internal audit involves internal control. While it doesn't have primary responsibility for establishing or maintaining the internal control system, internal audit plays an important role in evaluating the effectiveness of control. By monitoring how well risk management, internal control and governance processes are operating in a company, internal audit provides useful information to senior management and valuable support to the audit committee. Being operationally removed, internal audit can provide an objective view of the state of control.

The internal audit function also can help the audit committee conduct special studies or investigations on a range of issues, including potential or suspected fraud or irregularities. Many internal audit functions review company compliance with laws and regulations and with the code of conduct, areas audit committees commonly oversee.

The audit committee plays a key role in ensuring that internal audit is functioning effectively, by monitoring the activities discussed below, and establishing and maintaining an open line of communication with the internal audit director. Exhibit 3.1 at the end of this section summarizes our 1999 survey findings on committees' involvement.

Charter and Reporting Level

The Institute of Internal Auditors *Standards for the Professional Practice of Internal Auditing (Standards),* issued initially in 1978, are being revised to reflect the many changes in the profession since that time. The draft revised *Standards* suggest that the internal audit function should have its purpose, authority and responsibilities formally set forth in a charter, which should be reviewed and approved by the board, or the audit committee on behalf of the board.

As part of the charter review, the committee should be satisfied that the internal audit director reports at a high enough level in the company to ensure adequate independence and objectivity. The director should not report to an officer who is directly responsible for the activities being audited. For example, in companies with both a chief financial officer (CFO) and a controller who is the principal accounting officer, the internal audit director should report to the CFO or higher executive level. In some companies, the internal audit director reports to the chief executive officer. Where this is not the case, the director should have direct and unrestricted access to the CEO, including periodic meetings to discuss important findings. The National Association of Corporate Directors' 1999–2000 Public Company Governance Survey found internal auditor reporting relationships as follows:

- 29 percent to the audit committee or committee chair
- 26 percent to the CEO
- 5 percent to a board chair who is not the CEO
- 38 percent to the CFO

Experience shows that where internal audit reports to a management executive, often it has dotted line reporting to the audit committee.

Internal Audit Director

Audit committee review and concurrence in the appointment of the internal audit director helps ensure both operational independence and effectiveness of the internal audit function. The committee needs to be satisfied with the independence and objectivity of the director and that he or she has the competency and capability to provide effective leadership. In our 1999 survey, 70 percent of internal audit directors said their appointment by management is approved by the audit committee, 10 percent said the audit committee has joint responsibility with management and 3 percent said audit committees take full responsibility for the appointment. Audit committee chairs reported that 49 percent of their audit committees had the "ultimate authority" to *select* and *evaluate* the internal audit director.

The internal audit director walks a fine line—both a member of company management and also expected to report *on* company management. Accordingly, the director sometimes has a difficult task in serving the needs of the various stakeholders. The committee's ongoing dialogue with the internal audit director helps build a strong relationship and enables the committee to learn quickly of any potential problems with or restrictions on the function's work. Although the committee needs to monitor the process used to evaluate the director's performance, responses from internal audit directors indicate 34 percent of audit committees are not involved at all. On the other hand, 24 percent are extremely involved, with the remaining committees "moderately" involved.

Just as the audit committee should approve a hiring decision, it also should concur with a decision to replace the director. This is important to ensure such action doesn't represent an attempt by management to restrict the inquiries or findings of internal audit. Close involvement in and approval of a proposed removal decision also enable the committee to be informed by an outgoing director of systemic issues—which the committee can then investigate further.

Committee members should take note that 44 percent of internal audit directors said they believe company management could dismiss them without audit committee (or board) approval. Another 24 percent didn't know whether committee or board approval would be required. This represents a substantial perception of lack of board-level support, which could be critical when tough issues arise. Audit committees can give internal audit directors additional confidence to make the tough calls by assuring them that any move to replace them is subject to committee review and approval.

Audit Plans

The audit committee should review the planned scope of internal auditing activities for the year and determine that the internal audit director and management consider it appropriate and responsive to the level of risk within the company. The committee should be comfortable with internal audit involvement in areas such as key information systems, compliance with laws and regulations, and compliance with the corporate code of conduct. Many audit committees look at the potential audit universe—all the company's auditable units—and the coverage these units have received, focusing on frequency and extent of coverage and any gaps.

The committee should inquire about the degree to which internal auditing activities are coordinated with those of the external auditors. The goal should be to achieve effective and efficient audit coverage by coordinating, to the extent possible, audit coverage of the two groups.

Subsequently, the committee should review the extent to which audit plans were actually executed and reasons for significant deviations. The committee should be mindful that management might request internal audit to undertake special projects that, while well intended, could divert the function from important planned activities. Internal audit plans and staffing should be determined considering that special projects might be requested.

Budgets and Staffing

The committee should be satisfied, by inquiry of both management and the internal audit director, that the function's staffing and budget are adequate to allow it to effectively perform its responsibilities. The committee should review the quality of internal audit staff. One measure of quality is the number of professionally qualified staff, such as Certified Internal Auditors, Certified Public Accountants or Chartered Accountants, Certified Management Accountants, Certified Fraud Examiners and Certified Information Systems Auditors. If internal audit is involved in operational audits, participation of other specially qualified employees such as industrial engineers may be important. However, certifications or other academic or trade organization recognitions cannot substitute for keen business and industry knowledge, intellectual curiosity and persistence, and the ability to draw sound conclusions and to work effectively with, but independent of management.

The audit committee also should consider the level of continuing training and education, as well as continuity, of internal audit staff. Many companies use internal audit as a rotational or temporary assignment. This can provide a valuable training ground, but if the turnover rate is too high, effectiveness can be diminished—not only might there be periods of staff shortages, but the experience and "institutional memory" of the function could suffer. Conversely, an appropriate level of incoming new staff can bring needed technical skills and a fresh perspective. Rotational assignments sometimes are done at the director level, with some companies filling the director position from operational business units and rotating the role over a period such as three years.

A growing trend is the use of outside service providers to perform internal audit work. Potential benefits from partial or full outsourcing include:

- Access to specialized resources—especially in areas such as information systems or financial instruments
- Flexibility and the opportunity for the audit function to balance capacity—for example, when a new system is being implemented, allowing the development process to be audited without adding permanent resources
- Access to best practices and the ability to benchmark against other organizations
- Access to automated tools and technologies that an individual function might not be able to develop
- The opportunity for company management to focus on its core competencies

Those advantages, however, need to be weighed against the benefits of sourcing the internal auditing function within the company:

- Greater familiarity with corporate culture
- Training ground for management—not only giving future company leaders a grounding in risk management and control, but also exposing them to different business operations
- Ability to more closely control internal audit activities and retain organizational knowledge

Regulatory issues also may influence the company to maintain internal audit "in-house."

Audit Results

The internal audit director should report results of the function's auditing activities to the committee. Under normal circumstances, reporting is in summary form, but the audit committee should concur in the level of detail to be provided. Importantly, specific findings and recommendations relating to significant matters always should be reported to the committee. It is not uncommon for a committee also to specify timing, requiring vital issues to be reported immediately to the committee chair, without waiting for the next regular committee meeting.

Many committees review with internal audit the status of past findings—whether management has taken corrective action on significant recommendations and whether changes instituted are effective.

There is growing impetus for broad-based discussions with the audit committee, or perhaps the committee chair, on the state of the risk and control environment. Some audit committees look to the internal audit director, together with the external auditors, counsel, compliance officer, corporate security and other management, for periodic briefings providing an overview and opportunity to discuss corporate progress in dealing with issues.

Independence and Objectivity

The audit committee should be satisfied that internal audit maintains organizational independence and objectivity. Internal audit independence comprises absence of bias or undue influence regarding audit topics or findings. As noted, the director should report to an appropriate executive level in the organization. Through discussions with the director, management and the external auditors, the committee should ascertain whether internal audit has access to all areas of the company necessary for carrying out its responsibilities. Management and the external auditors also should be asked their views on internal audit's independence and objectivity. Frequent interaction of the committee with the internal audit director during the year gives the committee added insight into these issues.

Compliance with IIA *Standards*

The audit committee should ask the internal audit director whether internal auditing activities conform with the IIA's *Standards* or their equivalent. The committee might inquire whether the internal audit function has undergone an external quality assurance review and, if so, what findings arose and what actions were taken. The new draft *Standards* suggest that external quality reviews be conducted approximately every five years. Although a relatively small percentage of internal audit functions undertake these reviews, those doing so have found that such reviews can provide added assurance to the audit committee that the internal audit function remains effective.

Exhibit 3.1: Audit Committee Oversight of Internal Audit

	Frequency of Audit Committee Review				If Reviewed, Percentage Approved
	Never	Seldom	Occasionally	Frequently	
Charter and Updates	5%	17%	58%	19%	87%
Annual Plan	5%	2%	18%	75%	86%
Changes to Plan	17%	15%	31%	36%	69%
Adequacy of Staffing Levels	2%	7%	29%	61%	56%
Staff Qualifications	12%	22%	42%	19%	31%
Budget	29%	10%	31%	27%	44%
Audit Results	7%	2%	13%	78%	56%
Operational Independence	5%	12%	41%	36%	65%

Source: Director of Internal Auditing Survey

Relationship with the External Auditors

The objective of an external audit of financial statements is to determine whether, in the auditors' opinion, the financial statements present fairly, in all material respects, the company's financial position, results of operations and cash flows in conformity with generally accepted accounting principles.

Because the audit committee's primary interest is reliable financial reporting, it should communicate with the external auditors on an ongoing basis, paying particular attention to the:

- Proposed audit scope and approach
- Financial statements and audit findings
- Performance of the external auditors
- Independence of the external auditors
- Nature of special services provided by the external auditors

The audit committee should receive from the external auditors information on these matters as well as information that is the subject of required communications to the audit committee, discussed below. Additionally, the audit committee should utilize the knowledge and experience of the external auditors by meeting with them to receive updates on developments affecting financial reporting and other pertinent matters.

Selection and Evaluation

Since the external auditors review management's judgments and decisions, auditor selection should not be left entirely to management. Indeed, many audit committees have long been involved in approving the selection of auditors, with our 1999 survey showing 68 percent of audit committees have ultimate authority to select and evaluate the external auditors. Since then, such committee involvement has been put into rule. The New York Stock Exchange, National Association of Securities Dealers and American Stock Exchange amended their listing rules to highlight the audit committee's role in auditor selection, requiring a committee's charter to specify that the board and the audit committee—as the shareholders' representatives—have ultimate authority to select, evaluate and replace, if necessary, the external auditors.

In many companies, the shareholders ratify the selection of the external auditors. Because management is primarily responsible for financial reporting and will have day-to-day contact with the auditors, it should be a part of, and often initiates, the selection or reappointment process.

What should the committee look for in making its selection or reappointment decision? Consideration should be given to the firm's professional capabilities, reputation, resources and personnel assigned, effectiveness and efficiency of audit approach, and knowledge of the company's industry and geographic coverage. Also important is the quality of audit work performed, evidenced by matters such as identification and resolution of accounting and disclosure issues, recommendations on internal control and other opportunities for improvement, communication of information relevant to audit findings, and carrying out other professional responsibilities. Relevant as well are how adept the assigned personnel are in discussing, debating and successfully resolving difficult issues, and how well they relate to management and the audit committee. Some audit committees additionally look to the results of the firm's latest peer review, and the firm's involvement in any disciplinary action or litigation.

In addition to its own firsthand knowledge of these matters, the audit committee obtains management's feedback and recommendations on the auditors, and may seek the internal audit director's input on the quality of the external auditors' services.

Just as the committee has ultimate authority to make appointment and reappointment decisions, it should take ultimate responsibility for any dismissal. The committee should satisfy itself that any management-recommended dismissal doesn't result from legitimate positions taken by the external auditors. In the United States, when a public company's external auditors are dismissed or resign, management is required to file information about the change of auditors with the Securities and Exchange Commission detailing any disagreements with the auditors, and the auditors are required to submit a letter as to whether they agree with management's representations. The audit committee should ask the auditors whether, in their opinion, there are any disagreements to be reported, and should pay particular notice to auditor resignation as a bell-wether—potentially indicating deteriorating control conditions or poor reporting practices.

External Auditors' Independence

Independence enables auditors to act with integrity and objectivity. When the auditors are independent, their relationships, if any, with the company are not of a nature that would interfere with their ability to conduct the audit with an objective state of mind—for example, the auditors' judgments would not be swayed by personal financial interests, relatives' interests or joint business interests. And it's not only independence in fact that is important; the auditors must appear to be independent as well.

The importance of auditor independence and audit committee oversight is receiving increased attention. It has always been good practice for the external auditors to discuss their independence with the audit committee, and today this is required by professional and statutory rules in a number of countries. In the United States, the Independence Standards Board (ISB) was created to establish independence standards for auditors of public companies—to develop a conceptual framework for independence that will serve as the foundation for development of principles-based independence standards. In January 1999 the ISB issued Independence Standard No. 1, *Independence Discussions with Audit Committees*, requiring independence discussions between external auditors and the audit committee. Specifically, ISB No. 1 requires a public company's external auditors to, at least annually:

- Disclose in writing to the company's audit committee all relationships between the auditors and the company that, in the auditors' professional judgment, may reasonably be thought to bear on independence
- Confirm in writing that, in the auditors' professional judgment, they are independent of the company
- Discuss these matters with the audit committee

The auditing profession's guidance on ISB No. 1 recommends that external auditors also disclose the safeguards that are in place to prevent a lapse in independence from occurring.

Rules put in place by the major securities exchanges in the United States in 1999 parallel the above bulleted requirements, calling for audit committee charters to specify the committee's responsibilities in those areas. The rules also require that the charter specify the committee's responsibility for taking, or recommending that the full board take, appropriate action to oversee the external auditors' independence.

Examples of relationships to be discussed with the audit committee include family members of the auditing firm's partners and staff holding key positions with the company, former partners and staff employed by the company or serving on its board of directors, and nonaudit services provided to the company. Also, the American Institute of Certified Public Accountants (AICPA) Public Oversight Board (POB) Panel on Audit Effectiveness recommends in its 2000 report that the audit committee be advised of company plans to hire audit firm personnel into high-level positions and any actions to be taken to ensure that the auditors maintain independence.

The issue of providing consulting services to audit clients has received considerable attention over the years, and in some countries restrictions have been established. In the United States, for example, the SEC Practice Section of the AICPA prohibits certain services for SEC-registered audit clients, including conducting opinion polls, performing merger and acquisition services for a finder's fee, psychological testing, certain executive recruiting services and certain actuarial services for insurance companies.

Attention also has focused on other nonaudit service relationships between an auditor and an audit client and, in particular, the volume of those services, which some believe has a bearing on auditor independence. Although various studies have failed to demonstrate that nonaudit services delivered in accordance with professional and regulatory guidelines impair independence as such services increase, the perception issue continues to receive attention.

The SEC has been particularly active in the independence area and in 2000 proposed significant revisions to its existing auditor independence rules. Among other things, the proposal identifies certain nonaudit services, such as design and implementation of financial information systems and valuation and appraisal services, that auditors would not be allowed to provide to their audit clients. They also contain a requirement that companies disclose in their annual proxy statements information about the nonaudit services provided and the related fees charged by their auditors. The SEC is considering comments it has received on the proposal and the content of final rules remains to be seen.

The POB Panel on Audit Effectiveness recommends that audit committees preapprove nonaudit services to be offered by their auditors that exceed a threshold determined by the committee. The recommendation suggests audit committees consider matters such as any effects the service might have on audit effectiveness or on the quality and timeliness of the financial reporting process, whether the role of those performing the service would be inconsistent with the auditor's role, and whether a service performed by audit personnel would enhance their knowledge of the company's business and operations.

Audit committees have been focusing on the issue of nonaudit services, as evidenced by our survey where 94 percent of audit committee chairs said that the auditors' nonaudit services and fees are disclosed to the audit committee. Exhibit 3.2 shows how audit committee chairs view the relative importance of factors associated with nonaudit services.

Exhibit 3.2: Considering Auditor Independence and Nonaudit Services

Factors rated as extremely important

- Confidence in the audit engagement partner   82%

- Responsibility for the services is separate from the   65%
  audit engagement partner

- Nature of the services to be provided   62%

- Size of the fee for the services   38%

- Size of the fee for the services relative to the   38%
  audit fee

Source: Audit Committee Chair Survey

It remains to be seen what rules ultimately will be issued by the SEC and other regulators, and whether authoritative bodies will put the POB Panel's recommendations into rule. But certainly audit committees should be aware of the nature of nonaudit services provided by the external auditors, and the related fees. The committee should be satisfied that the auditors are complying with all applicable rules governing the nature of the nonaudit services provided, and should consider the impact, if any, of the nonaudit services on the auditors' objectivity.

Audit Scope

External auditors are responsible for determining the scope of the audit, based on a wide range of factors. The audit committee should consider the external auditors' assessment and decide whether the scope is appropriate for its needs. Some illustrative questions committee members may wish to ask the external auditors about the audit scope and approach include:

- What are the objectives of the audit?
- What are the company's financial reporting requirements and what is the expected timetable for meeting them?
- Which areas do you plan to emphasize in your audit and why?
- To what extent will you assess the company's internal control?
- How will this year's financial statements be affected by recent changes in accounting principles or regulatory requirements?

- How will any recent changes by the company, such as mergers and acquisitions, restructurings, a change of business strategy, a change of product lines, modification or amendments to a pension plan, financing arrangement or other unusual transactions, affect your audit or your report?
- How will your audit address the company's computer systems and applications?
- How will you coordinate your work with the internal auditors?
- What company locations will you visit this year? Do you rotate visits of company locations? If so, how do you determine which locations to visit and when?
- Which subsidiaries will you audit? What steps do you take for those not audited?
- If other auditing firms are involved, how will you satisfy yourself that their work is acceptable and that they are independent? Do you intend to refer to them in your report?
- What are your responsibilities with regard to detecting material errors, fraud and illegal acts?

Once the audit has been completed, the audit committee should ascertain whether it covered everything outlined in the original audit plan and the reason for any significant changes. Changes in scope may indicate unusual and unforeseen transactions or problems that occurred during the year.

Audit committee members are divided on the appropriate focus in reviewing the audit fee. Although some review the fee to ensure it is reasonable in relation to the amount of work the audit involved, most believe the main objective is to make sure the fee is sufficient to allow the external auditors to perform a competent audit. This is consistent with the POB's 1993 report, *In the Public Interest: Issues Confronting the Accounting Profession*, which recommended that "the audit committee or the board of directors should be satisfied that the audit fee negotiated by it or management for the entity's audit is sufficient to assure the entity will receive a comprehensive and complete audit." Obviously, the audit committee should object if the fee seems too high for the audit agreed upon, and the committee should expect the external auditors to be as productive as possible. But a committee that focuses on driving fees down does itself and the company a disservice.

A corollary recommendation comes from the POB Panel on Audit Effectiveness, suggesting the audit committee inquire about any time pressures on the auditor—including pressures on the timing of audit procedures, the degree of management cooperation and the potential effects on audit effectiveness.

Communications to the Audit Committee

Because of its importance, external auditors in some countries are required to make sure certain information is communicated to the board or its audit committee. This is the case in the United States, where communications are required by professional standards. While these communications may be by the auditors or management, written or oral, these matters must be communicated to the audit committee:

- *Auditors' responsibilities under generally accepted auditing standards*—Such matters as the auditors' responsibilities for internal control, whether the financial statements are free of material misstatement, the detection of fraud, and so forth. Often, these are set out in an engagement letter, which the committee should review, and in some cases the committee signs the letter on behalf of the company.

- *Significant accounting policies*—Initial selection of and changes in significant accounting policies or their application, methods used to account for significant unusual transactions, and effect of significant policies in controversial or emerging areas for which there is a lack of authoritative guidance or consensus.

- *Auditors' judgments about the quality of accounting principles*—The external auditors' views about the quality, not just acceptability, of the company's accounting principles and underlying estimates. Management, having primary responsibility for selecting and applying principles, should be an active participant in this discussion. The discussion should include matters of consistency of accounting policy application and clarity and completeness of the financial statements, including disclosures. It also should include items significantly impacting the representational faithfulness, verifiability and neutrality of accounting information provided in the financial statements. (This requirement applies only to SEC registrants and certain other companies.)

- *Management judgments and accounting estimates*—The process used by management in forming particularly sensitive accounting estimates and the basis for the external auditors' conclusions regarding the reasonableness of those estimates.

- *Audit adjustments*—All significant adjustments arising from the audit, whether or not recorded by the company, that could individually or in the aggregate have a significant effect on the financial statements. Additionally, consideration is given to whether an adjustment is indicative of a significant internal control deficiency that could cause interim or future financial reports to be materially misstated. And, the audit committee must be informed about uncorrected misstatements aggregated by the auditors and determined by management to be immaterial.

- *Other information in documents containing audited financial information*—The external auditors' responsibility for other information in documents containing audited financial statements, such as management's discussion and analysis and the board chair's letter. Also communicated are any procedures performed and the results. This responsibility often is referred to in the engagement letter.

- *Disagreements with management*—Any disagreements with management, whether or not satisfactorily resolved, about matters that individually or in the aggregate could be significant to the financial statements or auditors' report. Disagreements may arise over the application of accounting principles, basis for management's judgment concerning accounting estimates, scope of the audit, disclosures in the financial statements, or wording of the auditors' report. Disagreements do not include differences of opinion based on incomplete facts or preliminary information subsequently resolved.

- *Consultation with other independent accountants*—When management consults with other independent accountants about significant auditing and accounting matters.

- *Difficulties encountered in performing the audit*—Any serious difficulties encountered in dealing with management related to the performance of the audit.

- *Major issues discussed with management prior to retention*—Any major accounting, auditing or reporting issues discussed with management in connection with initial retention or reappointment of the external auditors, such as where the new auditors' viewpoint differs from the predecessor auditors'.
- *Significant deficiencies in internal control*—Any reportable conditions—significant deficiencies in the design or operation of internal control over financial reporting that came to the external auditors' attention.
- *Fraud and illegal acts*—Fraud involving senior management or causing a material misstatement of the financial statements, where the auditor determines there is evidence that such fraud may exist. Also, any illegal acts coming to the auditors' attention involving senior management and any other illegal acts, unless clearly inconsequential, should be communicated. If the company doesn't take appropriate remedial action with respect to an illegal act, the external auditors also may be required to report the matter to the SEC.

Audit committees should expect to receive communications on all of these matters, even if only to indicate there are no matters to report. When reported by management, the auditors' responsibility is to be satisfied with the completeness of the communication.

Management Representation Letter

The external auditors customarily request that management provide written representation on such matters as the collectibility of receivables, realizability of inventory, significant events that occurred after the balance sheet date and knowledge of illegal acts. The external auditors also will ask management to comment on other important matters such as whether reserves for specific matters are reasonable and whether specified intangible assets can be realized. The purpose of the letter is to confirm oral representations given to the external auditors, document the continued appropriateness of the representations and reduce the possibility of a misunderstanding.

Committee members should be aware that the letter exists, and might want to inquire of the auditors whether there are unusual matters discussed therein and whether they are being handled correctly. The audit committee also might ask the auditors whether there were any difficulties in obtaining any representation; such difficulties could point to particularly sensitive areas requiring further committee inquiry.

Use of Other Auditors

Occasionally, a firm other than the company's principal external auditor is engaged to perform audits of some of the company's subsidiaries or equity investments. Generally, the reasons for this are quite logical, for example, when the principal auditor does not have an office convenient to a subsidiary location, or a subsidiary was recently acquired and its former auditor is completing the audit in the acquisition year. Poor service or excessive fees also could be legitimate reasons to use other auditors. Or, the company might be a party to a joint venture, and the auditors for the other investor(s) may be auditing the joint venture. However, there have been instances where management's involvement of other auditors was due to an ulterior motive. The audit committee should ask whether firms other than the principal auditors are used, understand the rationale behind the decision, and obtain reports from the other auditors on their independence, similar to the report received from the principal auditors.

Second Opinions

Occasionally, a company may ask a second firm of independent accountants for advice. This would be appropriate when the company is involved in matters where generally accepted accounting principles are unsettled or the other firm has addressed a unique or new transaction (for example, a novel financial instrument). The purpose of employing a second firm may be to confirm the advice of its own accounting firm or possibly to gain additional insights into a position taken by the other firm under apparently similar circumstances. Although a company might be "opinion shopping," the usual reason for a second opinion is simply to ensure that the company is following an appropriate policy. Whatever the reason, the audit committee should be familiar with the situation. Additionally, for public companies in the United States that change auditors, the required SEC filing must describe consultations with the incoming auditors on any second opinions sought during the previous two years.

Auditors' Access to the Audit Committee

Internal and external auditors are critical resources supporting the audit committee in carrying out its activities and meeting its responsibilities. To maximize effectiveness, both audit groups must have direct and unrestricted access to the committee. Leveraging this access and having it work requires effort on all sides—not only must the auditors be willing to talk candidly to the committee, but the committee must make it clear it welcomes their views. Accordingly, the audit committee chair should instruct both the internal audit director and the external auditors that it expects to be advised of any areas requiring the committee's attention—and be receptive to their communications.

Audit committee meetings provide the most common opportunity for such access. Our 1993 survey showed that roughly 90 percent of both internal audit directors and external auditors attended committee meetings, and our 1999 survey shows 93 percent of internal audit directors attending all regular meetings, with the rest attending at least one a year. Not only does attendance allow the auditors to build a strong professional relationship and develop trust with the committee, it also enables them to identify and respond to emerging issues or committee concerns.

Best practice demands that the audit committee meet in separate private sessions with the internal audit director and the external auditors. These private meetings are important in enhancing and protecting the independence of both auditing groups.

Ideally, these private meetings should be scheduled and held routinely, whether or not the director of internal auditing, external auditors or committee members believe there are specific matters that require such a meeting. This avoids potential difficulties that may arise when there are matters that must be discussed privately and a formal request for such a meeting must be made. If the audit committee decides private sessions with each audit group are not necessary at every committee meeting, it should ensure such meetings are held at least annually. And, there should be an open communications channel with the audit committee chair so that an interim private meeting may be arranged if needed. Chapter 7 indicates the extent to which these private meetings occur.

What gets discussed at these meetings? The discussion with the internal audit director includes the quality of financial and accounting personnel, performance of the external auditors, the director's principal concerns and matters of concern to committee members. The external auditors routinely discuss such matters as the quality of the company's accounting and financial personnel, performance of the internal auditing function, external auditors' principal concerns and any other matters the external auditors or committee members wish to discuss.

It is important that the internal and external auditors and committee members be completely candid during these sessions. Whenever sensitive issues are raised, the committee should probe to see if the risks might be larger than they first appear. Discussions in private sessions afford committee members an excellent opportunity to surface issues. To this end, one committee chair noted his favorite question of auditors in an executive session: "Even though you're satisfied with the audit results and have told us there are no significant matters to bring to our attention, what is it about this company that concerns you the most?"

CHAPTER 4
COMMITTEE COMPOSITION

Having the right directors on the audit committee—those with the requisite knowledge, judgment, independence and other attributes, including level of commitment—is key to ensuring that the committee's responsibilities are carried out effectively.

Selecting Committee Members

Shareholder groups, institutional investors, regulators and others continue to apply pressure for improved audit committee performance, with member selection being a key focus. Best practice suggests that audit committee members be appointed by the board of directors or a nominating committee comprised solely of independent board members. Because the audit committee's principal function is that of management oversight, most observers believe having the CEO appoint new committee members could compromise the committee's independence or result in superior candidates being excluded from consideration.

The National Association of Corporate Directors' (NACD) 1999–2000 Public Company Governance Survey shows that in 41 percent of companies, audit committee members are chosen by the full board, while in 24 percent they are chosen by a nominating committee. The CEO and/or board chair selects committee members in 35 percent of respondent companies. Practice is somewhat different internationally, with Exhibit 4.1 showing how respondents to our 1999 survey choose new committee members. Note that respondents from companies where the role of board chair is combined with that of chief executive—typical in the United States—used the "chair" designation; and we understand that many respondents listed "other" for selection by the full board.

Exhibit 4.1: Who Appoints New Audit Committee Members?

Board chair	39%
Nominating committee	29%
CEO	0%
Audit committee chair	0%
Other	32%

Source: Audit Committee Chair Survey

Although the audit committee chair and the CEO might not be directly involved in selecting new committee members, they may be consulted. As board members, they have an opportunity to offer views on prospective candidates, and the committee chair in particular may have important insight into skill sets that should be sought in a new member to supplement the committee's existing strengths.

Members' Attributes

Documented qualification requirements for audit committee members can be useful in selecting new members, particularly when they include information as to required level of expertise in financial matters. But our 1999 survey shows only 20 percent of audit committees have a written description of qualifications to use in the selection decision. Such a description provides particularly useful guidance to the directors tasked with selecting new members, especially if new directors are being recruited to the board with the express intention they will serve on the audit committee.

Whether new board members should be selected to serve on the audit committee is a matter of debate. A drawback is that a new board member would have to learn about both the company and its financial reporting processes at the same time. On the other hand, the scope of audit committee oversight provides an excellent venue for a new director to learn about the company. Boards that assign new directors to the audit committee should make sure there are enough experienced directors on the committee and that new members receive effective orientation.

A good understanding of the business, including its products and services and the company's industry, is essential, as it enables members to assess the appropriateness of accounting principles and financial results. Antitrust provisions in some countries, however, make it difficult to recruit a director with existing in-depth industry knowledge. Members who have limited familiarity with the company's industry should be thoroughly briefed as part of their orientation. Such knowledge may be deemed vital. In the United States, for example, the Federal Deposit Insurance Corporation Improvement Act requires that audit committees of "large" insured depository institutions include members with banking or related financial management expertise.

Directors must plan to dedicate substantial time and energy if they agree to audit committee service. They should be willing to devote the time necessary to become familiar with the financial reporting process, prepare for and attend meetings, and participate otherwise as needed. Members also need to commit to the ongoing training and development they may need to maintain and enhance their individual and collective effectiveness, including education about the company's business and industry. This willingness to commit the time needed is increasingly important as the demands on audit committee members increase. Indeed, audit committee members may need to limit the number of directorships they hold so they can meet the demands of their audit committee responsibilities.

Other attributes committee members should possess are:

- Extremely high level of integrity.
- Recognition of the committee's significant role.
- Knowledge of the company's risks and controls and the ability to offer informed insights— this knowledge may be developed after the director has joined the committee.
- Inquisitiveness and independent judgment—asking the right questions and ably interpreting the answers.
- Ability to offer new perspectives and constructive suggestions.

In selecting a committee chair, the board of directors should choose someone with the requisite characteristics, including strong leadership qualities, objectivity and the ability to promote effective working relationships—among committee members, management, and internal and external auditors.

Two additional attributes of committee members—financial knowledge and independence—are particularly significant.

Financial Knowledge

As the board committee that oversees financial reporting and the audit functions, a good understanding of financial reporting is clearly important for audit committee members. The importance of this understanding has been reflected in rule—for example, the New York Stock Exchange (NYSE), National Association of Securities Dealers (NASD) and American Stock Exchange (AMEX) require that all audit committee members be "financially literate." The NYSE leaves the definition to the board, while the NASD and AMEX rules describe literacy as the ability to read and understand fundamental financial statements, including a company's balance sheet, income statement and cash flow statement. Pragmatically, the rules recognize that new committee members may lack such knowledge, and allow them a reasonable period of time after appointment to the committee to develop it.

The NYSE, NASD and AMEX also require that at least one audit committee member have accounting or financial management "expertise." Here, too, the NYSE leaves interpretation to the board, whereas the NASD and AMEX rules describe this member as having past employment experience in finance or accounting, requisite professional certification in accounting or other comparable experience or background that results in the individual's financial sophistication, including being or having been a chief executive officer, chief financial officer or other senior officer with financial oversight responsibilities.

The American Society of Corporate Secretaries, in its 1998 Survey on Audit Committee Effectiveness, found 74 percent of respondents had at least one audit committee member who had a finance or accounting background.

Regardless of applicable rules, audit committee members need sufficient knowledge of accounting and financial reporting to enable them to understand the financial reporting process, financial statements and related business issues to carry out the committee's charge. With increasing complexity of business transactions and accounting and reporting principles and practices, members need to be positioned to ask the right questions and probe and challenge as necessary. A candid self-assessment and peer assessment of members' financial knowledge is an effective first step in determining this knowledge level and can point to areas where supplementary training and development are needed.

Independence

The audit committee is responsible for overseeing the financial reporting process, and in doing so, it often must question the judgment of management or take positions that may be contrary to those of management. It must act in the interest of the shareholders. Because of this oversight role, there is no doubt that independence is essential for an audit committee to function effectively.

Having a fully independent audit committee doesn't, by itself, ensure that the committee will be effective. But having a committee on which members are beholden to management greatly increases the likelihood that it won't be, as members might be reluctant to ask necessary questions and persist until they get needed answers. Therefore, a committee composed of all independent directors is optimal—and clearly best practice. Such directors are in a much better position to provide the objective point of view crucial to a committee's effectiveness.

How should independence be defined for audit committee members? Many organizations have developed rules or definitions to guide companies, and these can be useful in setting the committee's independence guidelines. It's important to recognize, however, that a director who technically meets the letter of an independence rule might still not be independent if other factors prevent that director from exercising true objectivity. The ultimate goal is member independence and objectivity in mind and action—rules and guidelines can serve only to help select and retain the right members.

In 1994, following extensive research and review of legal precedents, the American Law Institute (ALI) issued its influential *Principles of Corporate Governance: Analysis and Recommendations*. ALI recommends that the audit committee "should be comprised exclusively of directors who are neither employed by the corporation nor were so employed within the two preceding years." It also calls for at least a majority of members having no significant relationship with the corporation's senior executives. It describes "significant relationships" as including situations in which the director:

- Is a member of the immediate family of an individual who is or was an officer of the company during the current year or preceding two years.

- In either of the last two years, paid to or received from the company commercial payment exceeding $200,000, or owned or could vote an equity interest in a business organization which paid to or received from the company amounts which, when multiplied by the director's percentage equity interest in the company, exceeded $200,000.
- Is a principal manager of a business organization to which the company paid, or from which the company received, during either of the two preceding years, commercial payments exceeding the greater of 5 percent of the organization's consolidated gross revenues, or $200,000.
- Is affiliated in a professional capacity with a law firm that was the company's primary legal advisor on corporate law or securities matters, or with an investment banking firm retained by the company as advisor or managing underwriter in an issue of the its securities, within the two preceding years, or was so affiliated with such a firm.

In using these guidelines, consideration should be given to the fact that the monetary amounts presented are in 1994 dollars. Also, the guidelines provide an exception, noting that "if, on the basis of countervailing or other special circumstances, it could not reasonably be believed that the judgment of a person in the director's position would be affected by the relationship (in the last three bullets, above) in a manner adverse to the corporation," then the director won't be deemed to have a significant relationship. Thus, the ALI guidelines provide for judgment in determining whether a director is free of significant relationships.

Other influential definitions of independence were incorporated into the rules issued in 1999 by the NYSE, NASD and AMEX. For example, the NYSE rules require that all audit committee members be independent, having "no relationship to the company that may interfere with the exercise of their independence from management and the company." Exhibit 4.2 outlines which types of relationships would prevent a director from being considered independent under the NYSE rules.

Notwithstanding the specific NYSE rules, in limited circumstances the board of directors is permitted to apply its business judgment to allow a director not considered independent due to the three-year restriction period for employees or immediate family, to serve on the audit committee. Any such exception, however, requires subsequent proxy disclosure.

The NASD and AMEX rules differ slightly, but generally parallel the thrust of the NYSE rules. For example, one difference is that the NASD/AMEX rules apply a specific dollar limit to the amount of compensation a director could receive for nonboard services before having independence impaired. The board override provisions also differ slightly.

In the United States, the Securities and Exchange Commission (SEC) rules adopted in 1999 require companies to disclose in their proxy statements whether the audit committee members are "independent" as defined in the applicable listing standards and to disclose certain information regarding any director on the audit committee who is not "independent." SEC registrants not subject to the NYSE, NASD or AMEX listing rules also must disclose in their proxy

---

Exhibit 4.2: NYSE Rules on Independence

- *Employees.* A director who is an employee (including non-employee executive officers) of the company or any of its affiliates may not serve on the audit committee until three years following the termination of his or her employment. In the event the employment relationship is with a former parent or predecessor of the company, the director could serve on the audit committee after three years following the termination of the relationship between the company and the former parent or predecessor.
- *Business Relationship.* A director (i) who is a partner, controlling shareholder, or executive officer of an organization that has a business relationship with the company, or (ii) who has a direct business relationship with the company (e.g., a consultant) may serve on the audit committee only if the company's Board of Directors determines in its business judgment that the relationship does not interfere with the director's exercise of independent judgment. In making a determination regarding the independence of a director pursuant to this paragraph, the Board of Directors should consider, among other things, the materiality of the relationship to the company, to the director, and, if applicable, to the organization with which the director is affiliated.
  "Business relationships" can include commercial, industrial, banking, consulting, legal, accounting and other relationships. A director can have this relationship directly with the company, or the director can be a partner, officer or employee of an organization that has such a relationship. The director may serve on the audit committee without such board determination after three years following the termination of, as applicable, either: (1) the relationship between the organization with which the director is affiliated and the company; (2) the relationship between the director and his or her partnership status, shareholder interest or executive officer position; or (3) the direct business relationship between the director and the company.
- *Cross Compensation Committee Link.* A director who is employed as an executive of another corporation where any of the company's executives serves on that corporation's compensation committee may not serve on the audit committee.
- *Immediate Family.* A director who is an immediate family member of an individual who is an executive officer of the company or any of its affiliates cannot serve on the audit committee until three years following the termination of such employment relationship.

---

statements whether, if they have an audit committee, the members are "independent" and which of the three definitions of independence was used.

Other countries have issued similar recommendations for independence. The Cadbury Committee in the United Kingdom recommended that audit committee membership be confined to nonexecutive directors, the majority of whom are to be independent of the company. The Toronto Stock Exchange Committee on Corporate Governance in Canada (the Dey Committee) proposed that audit committees be composed only of outside directors.   The Australian Investment Managers' Association, in its *Corporate Governance — A Guide for Investment Managers and Corporations*, recommended that the audit committee be chaired by an independent director and be composed entirely of nonexecutive directors, a majority of whom should be independent.

The impact of share ownership on independence is another issue subject to considerable debate. Should there be share holding limits for committee members? At first glance, it appears that how much stock a member holds should be irrelevant, because the committee's basic charge is to protect shareholders' interests. Indeed, many corporate governance thought leaders believe that a substantial share ownership by directors better aligns their interests with those of shareholders, and, indeed, some companies pay a substantial part of directors' fees in company stock or options. However, there certainly might be circumstances where having a large financial interest could be a problem; for example, a director owning a large amount of company stock might attempt to unduly influence other members of the committee. Although shareholdings, in and of themselves, normally would not seem to impair one's ability to serve as an audit committee member, the full board should consider at what stage shareholdings could have that effect. In some industries—banking, for example—there are often specific prohibitions against large shareholders being members of an audit committee.

Recent evidence suggests that boards are making good progress on audit committee independence. The NACD's 1999–2000 Public Company Governance Survey found that 90 percent of CEOs considered their audit committees to be fully independent, up from 81 percent in 1995. And in our 1999 survey, all audit committee chairs said they believe that all their committee members are independent.

Because of disparity in definitions and guidelines, the board and the audit committee should agree on an appropriate definition of independence to apply to members. The definition should, of course, encompass any legal, listing or regulatory requirements applicable to the company. And, the board should monitor ongoing compliance. Also, it is useful for members periodically to assess their "true" independence—that is, their ability to exercise judgment freely and objectively in carrying out the committee's responsibilities.

Membership Term

When considering length of service on the committee, companies and boards need to balance the benefits of having experienced members oversee these complex activities, against the risk that, after extended service, some members may become stale or complacent. Some companies establish term limits to address this issue. Others believe the normal turnover of committee members solves this problem.

The American Society of Corporate Secretaries' (ASCS) survey of public companies found that only 5 percent have term limits for audit committee members. When there is no policy of mandatory rotation, it becomes more important that individual committee member performance be evaluated regularly. Such evaluations provide a mechanism for replacing members whose performance does not meet the board's or committee's expectations.

Whether or not a formal rotation policy for committee members exists, effective practice demands that the board, when planning for committee membership succession, consider both continuity and the desirability of a fresh perspective. Astute boards also monitor committee continuity, recognizing that rapid turnover can be detrimental to the committee's effectiveness, since members need time to understand technical issues and learn the committee's procedures. By monitoring to ensure that all experienced members don't depart from the committee within a short timeframe, the board protects newer members from being left without experienced guidance and historical perspective. Some boards stagger the terms of service for committee members, to help ensure this balance is maintained. Any service term requirements should be included in the committee's charter.

Committee Size

What is optimum committee size? In its 1994 Principles of Corporate Governance, the American Law Institute said audit committees should consist of at least three members. Similarly, the NYSE, NASD, and AMEX require that audit committees consist of at least three directors, and the Cadbury Committee recommended the same for UK publicly listed companies.

If there's a minimum, is there an upper limit on membership? Having more than three members provides a broader experience base, which can be valuable when addressing all aspects of the committee's mandate. But large committees may be unwieldy and make it difficult to keep meetings focused. They also may reduce the responsibility individual members feel, as one member might presume another will surely pick up on a troubling issue.

There is growing support for audit committees of three to six members. This range allows for active participation while keeping the size manageable. It also allows for a degree of continuity. In its 1998 Survey on Audit Committee Effectiveness, the ASCS found that over 80 percent of respondents had audit committees of between three and six members. Ultimately, though, the size of a particular committee must be appropriate for the company and its circumstances.

CHAPTER 5
TRAINING AND RESOURCES

Certain attributes that make an effective audit committee member—integrity, diligence, inquisitiveness and sound judgment, to name a few—are intrinsic qualities. But others, such as knowledge of financial reporting and the company's financial systems, aren't. Audit committee members need such knowledge to supplement their core attributes with the skills needed to do the job well.

Need for Training

Clearly, effective training is critical to enable audit committee members to thoroughly understand their responsibilities and develop the technical knowledge to discharge them effectively, but our 1993 survey found training was not widely provided.

Unfortunately, the intervening period has not seen substantial progress. In its 1998 Survey on Audit Committee Effectiveness, the American Society of Corporate Secretaries (ASCS) found that only 6 percent of 550 public companies provide formal training to audit committee members. And our 1999 survey found 46 percent of audit committee chairs saying specifically that their committee members need more continuing education, with more than one-third less than satisfied that their committee received appropriate training in:

- Accounting and financial reporting developments
- The company's business environment
- Key information systems, processes and controls in the company
- Enterprise-wide risk management concepts

In 1999, the Blue Ribbon Committee (BRC) recommended that audit committee members recognize the significance of their responsibilities and commit to undertaking associated training and development. Recommending that all audit committee members be financially literate, the BRC pointed to the use of training programs for those committee members with limited familiarity with financial reporting.

Meeting the Need

Audit committee members obtain needed knowledge from three main sources:

- Interfacing with management and other board members in carrying out their board responsibilities
- Independent reading
- Formal training programs

It appears that too frequently, however, committee members find themselves relying on the first, having little time for the second and failing to carve out the requisite time for the third. With the ever-increasing complexity of issues with which they need to deal, audit committee members are well served to insist on receiving and to devote the time necessary to formal training sessions, ensuring they have sufficient up-to-date and relevant knowledge to do the job well.

Two main types of formal training can help meet audit committee members' development needs. The first provides new members the requisite background, process knowledge and financial literacy. The second enables all members to update their knowledge of the business and reporting requirements, and address changes in committee responsibilities—essentially ongoing education.

New Member Orientation

New members joining the committee have special needs. They need to understand the committee's roles and responsibilities and expectations placed on them, and to quickly become conversant with major processes and risks associated with financial reporting.

Many companies have formal orientation programs, as reported in Exhibit 5.1.

Exhibit 5.1: Existence of Orientation Programs

	Orientation programs for new audit committee members
North America	62%
Asia Pacific	30%
All Respondents	49%

Source: Audit Committee Chair Survey

To be effective—to know what questions to ask and how to interpret and follow up on answers—audit committee members must have a solid understanding of the business and related risks, as well as the committee's responsibilities. Orientation programs designed to meet these needs cover topics such as:

- *The committee's charter:* An outline of the committee's key responsibilities and any limits to its authority
- *Meeting schedule and agendas:* Meeting frequency, length and expected coverage
- *Business and industry:* Insight into strategy, competitive positioning, operations, sales channels, supply chain and other business issues, as a basis for recognizing and analyzing controls and reported results
- *Key risks:* In both the business and the financial reporting process
- *Key financial reporting, operations and compliance controls:* The control environment, security and integrity of information systems, and how management addresses key risks
- *Standard financial reports:* What information flows through to financial reports, what key line items represent and how to read reports and recognize issues
- *Key accounting policies:* What they are, why they were selected and what impact they have on financial reports
- *Statutory and regulatory requirements:* Identity and nature of externally imposed requirements and description and background of current issues, including requirements placed on audit committee itself, as well as on the company
- *Reporting and audit processes:* Overview of how financial reports are developed and how management, the committee and auditors work to ensure reliability
- *Earnings trends:* Financial position and prospects of company
- *Support and resources:* Who supports the committee
- *Internal auditing:* Responsibilities, reporting relationship with the committee, nature of audit plans, reports
- *External auditors:* Relationship with the committee, audit scope, reports
- *Committee assessment:* Self-assessment and charter review processes

Company management and internal audit often are well placed to provide information and orientation training, as are external auditors, who can offer a valuable perspective on the financial reporting process, their role and their view of key risks. Even experienced audit committee members find it useful to receive orientation materials periodically, so they can both understand what new members are learning and fill gaps in their knowledge.

Audit committee members also benefit from attending company-sponsored training programs or programs available from professional organizations. Such programs can be particularly useful for committee members needing to achieve financial literacy quickly.

Ongoing Development

Audit committee members, including experienced ones, need continuing information and training to allow them to stay current with both the implications of significant changes in the company—such as acquisitions or expansion into new lines of business—and developments in accounting and financial reporting. Accordingly, many topics covered will depend on the company's business and external developments. Additionally, training is required when the committee's responsibilities increase—for example, if the committee assumes oversight of enterprise-wide risk management, legal and regulatory compliance, or compliance with the code of conduct.

Among the more important ongoing information needs are:

- Regular updates on developments in accounting and reporting standards promulgated by standard setters such as the Financial Accounting Standards Board or regulators such as the Securities and Exchange Commission. To be most relevant, these briefings should be limited to matters most likely to impact the company. The committee should be made aware of impending changes in standards, how they will affect the company and how management plans to deal with them.
- Periodic briefings by the company's business units on operational as well as financial reporting. This helps committee members understand and anticipate and assess business units' financial results. Such briefings are particularly relevant when a company has acquired or expanded into new businesses, or shifted its strategic focus. Some committee members find it enlightening to hold these meetings at operating locations.
- Briefings on key support departments or cross-business unit issues. These are useful, particularly when significant changes are underway. Subjects include new information systems implementation or risks and controls surrounding e-commerce.
- Targeted sessions on special risk areas. These are particularly helpful for committees of companies operating in specialized industries. For example, audit committees of financial institutions benefit from briefings on controls in technical areas such as foreign currency trading and financial derivatives. Similarly, audit committees of e-commerce companies benefit from sessions on how the company is ensuring system availability and protecting the privacy and confidentiality of customers' personal information.
- Sessions on changing corporate governance standards, particularly as they relate to the audit committee itself. Proposed rules need to be explained to members, so they can proactively consider actions needed.

These ongoing development and education sessions sometimes occur as part of a regular committee meeting—included on the agenda—but this requires extending normal meeting duration. Separate sessions are beneficial in providing adequate time and focus apart from the committee's ongoing responsibilities. The selected venue may depend on the number of participants (entire committee versus certain members) and logistical issues in assembling the committee for a separate session.

In our 1999 survey, audit committee chairs identified management and external auditors as the two groups best positioned to provide continuing education. While most training is likely to be provided by these two groups, committee members may identify outside seminars and conferences meeting their development needs.

Resources

Best practice demands that audit committees be furnished with adequate resources needed to fulfill their responsibilities. The most obvious and frequent resource required is administrative assistance, invariably provided by the company. Generally, the committee looks to the corporate secretary or internal audit director to provide or coordinate the necessary administrative support, which typically includes distributing agendas and briefing materials before meetings, producing minutes, and obtaining information and interfacing with members of management as needed.

Audit committees require additional resources for special situations. For example, when faced with a possible fraud, the audit committee may initiate a special investigation and engage special counsel and forensic accountants to assist.

The 1998 ASCS survey found that over three-quarters of audit committees have the right to hire outside advisors at their discretion. Common and best practice is for committee charters to specifically empower the committee to engage whatever resources, including counsel, it deems necessary to fulfill its responsibilities. Many audit committees use the services of outside specialists or advisors such as special counsel, consulting accountants, environmental engineers or valuation specialists, depending on the specific need.

CHAPTER 6
CHARTER, EVALUATION, REPORTING

To successfully discharge their responsibilities, audit committees must understand exactly what those responsibilities are. There needs to be clear agreement with the board on scope, avoiding misunderstandings or gaps in overall board oversight. And to operate at peak performance, the committee should monitor its own effectiveness, identifying improvement needs and opportunities. The audit committee also may, in today's corporate governance environment, find it beneficial, or in some cases required, to report to shareholders on its activities.

Charter

Once the audit committee has determined its responsibilities and how it will organize to discharge its duties, it should capture those decisions in a written charter or terms of reference document. This:

- Confirms the scope of the committee's duties, both for the committee and the full board
- Guides agenda setting for committee meetings
- Provides checkpoints for the committee, allowing it to track activities against the charter
- Outlines for new members the committee's responsibilities, providing important orientation information

An effective charter clearly defines the committee's purpose and scope of its responsibilities, covering:

- Purpose/mission
- Composition: size and member attributes, e.g., independence and financial knowledge
- Frequency and timing of meetings
- Roles and responsibilities
- Relationship with management and internal and external auditors
- Reporting responsibilities
- Authority to conduct special investigations

The charter should be reviewed and approved, and revised as necessary, by the full board. The board should strive to avoid unduly restricting the committee, because the committee requires sufficient flexibility to operate effectively. It is particularly important, for example, that the charter stipulate the committee's authority to conduct any special investigation it believes is required to fulfill its responsibilities, including its right to engage resources. The charter may be a bylaw provision, a board resolution or any other written document.

The importance of a written charter has long been recognized by many committees, and increasingly has been incorporated into guidance and rules. In 1992, the Cadbury Committee recommended that audit committees have a written charter, and in 1999, the New York Stock Exchange (NYSE), National Association of Securities Dealers (NASD) and American Stock Exchange (AMEX) issued rules requiring listed companies to adopt a formal written charter. These rules require charters to specify:

- Scope of the committee's responsibilities and how it carries them out, including structure, process and membership requirements
- Committee responsibility for ensuring it obtains from the external auditors a formal written statement delineating all relationships between the auditors and the company, and its responsibility for discussing with the auditors any disclosed relationships or services that may impact auditor objectivity and independence
- Committee responsibility for taking, or recommending that the full board take, appropriate action to oversee independence of the external auditors
- External auditors' ultimate accountability to the board and audit committee, which have the ultimate authority and responsibility to select, evaluate and, where appropriate, replace them

The audit committee charter should be a living document. The board should see that the charter responds to the company's particular needs and, as those needs change, so should the charter. Indeed, the NYSE, NASD and AMEX rules require that audit committees review and reassess their charter's adequacy annually.

In related rules, also adopted in 1999, the Securities and Exchange Commission (SEC) requires registered companies to disclose in their proxy statements whether the audit committee has adopted a formal written charter. If so, the charter must be attached to the proxy statement at least every third year.

In our 1999 survey, 94 percent of audit committee chairs report their committees have adopted a charter. The National Association of Corporate Directors' (NACD) 1999–2000 Public Company Governance Survey found that 71 percent of respondents' audit committees have written charters. Both surveys were conducted before the new rules took effect.

Appendix B contains a sample charter. It is presented for illustrative purposes and needs to be tailored to meet an organization's needs. As the new SEC disclosure rules take effect, additional examples of charters will be found in proxy statements.

Evaluating the Committee

The audit committee should evaluate its performance regularly, to ensure it continues to meet expectations of the committee members themselves, the full board and other stakeholders. There are several ways to evaluate performance.

- *Compare committee's activities against its charter.* Our 1999 survey shows, of audit committees that have adopted a charter, 71 percent self-assess their performance against it at least annually. An evaluation helps the committee confirm it has properly completed the full scope of its responsibilities during the year. Done in a timely manner, it allows the committee to take remedial steps in the event an item was missed. For efficiency, the evaluation might be scheduled at the same time the committee reassesses its charter.

- *Compare committee's activities against formal guidelines and rules.* Evaluating how well the committee's activities reflect recommendations from bodies such as the Cadbury Committee, Blue Ribbon Committee and NACD's Blue Ribbon Commission on Audit Committees is another evaluative approach. This helps ensure that the committee focuses on emerging changes in expectations. Although not all recommendations necessarily apply to or are suitable for every audit committee, understanding them and evaluating whether and how they might be applied can be a valuable exercise. Our 1999 survey found that 66 percent of audit committees benchmark their activities against such recommendations. Done proactively, benchmarking allows committees to compare their practices with draft guidance and proposed rules to identify any gaps early and craft desired changes.

- *Compare committee's activities against best practice.* Benchmarking against best practice is another effective way to improve committee performance, and includes approaches proved effective that typically go beyond formal guidelines and rules. In addition to this report, sources of best practice information include published surveys and studies, members of the company's management (especially those individuals serving on other companies' audit committees) and external and internal auditors. Included as Appendix A is a self-assessment guide that allows committees to compare their activities against the leading practices described in this report.

Typically, a combination of approaches provides the committee with an appropriately broad spectrum. In particular, simply measuring activities performed against the charter might not ensure a committee's effectiveness. For instance, committee dynamics—communication, mutual trust and discussion time—not often covered in a charter, also have a significant impact on how well the committee does its job.

Some of the most effective audit committees assess the performance of not only the committee as a whole, but also individual members. Individual performance assessments look at members' objectivity and independence, insight, tenacity, judgment, communication skills, understanding of the company's business, understanding of and commitment to the duties and responsibilities of the committee, willingness to devote the time necessary to prepare for and participate in the committee's deliberations, and attendance at meetings. How is such an evaluation carried out?

Some committees have members self-assess personal performance and discuss results with the audit committee chair. Other committees have anonymous peer evaluations, which are compiled, reported to the chair, then discussed with members individually. Still others have the committee chair assess individual member performance. Increasingly, audit committees call on outside consultants to assist with the evaluation process—allowing the confidential capture of views and benchmarking against best practice.

How often are these assessments undertaken? Some committees perform evaluations annually, others less frequently—a wide range of variations exist. For example, some committees evaluate their activities against the charter annually, but assess individual member performance every two or three years. Benchmarking against best practice sometimes is done every three years, and against any new rule or guideline drafts when released. Circumstances dictate a need for more frequent reviews if, for example, the results of an assessment indicate significant shortfall in performance, in which case a follow-up review is appropriate.

Whatever the assessment method or frequency, the objective is to improve committee effectiveness. Accordingly, it is critical that evaluations focus not only on *what* the committee does, but also on *how effectively* the committee conducts its activities. If evaluations are performed well and documented, they can demonstrate to the board and others the committee's diligence in meeting its responsibilities.

The committee should review its results with the full board so that appropriate action can be taken on any recommendations resulting from the reviews. For example, results could indicate an additional skill set is needed, in which case board action would be required.

Reporting on Committee Activities

To the Board of Directors

Because the board delegates responsibilities to the audit committee, the board normally wants to be apprised of committee activities, including the extent to which the responsibilities were successfully discharged, key issues addressed and the committee's conclusions and recommendations. Most audit committees periodically report to the full board on their activities. While reporting formality, detail and frequency vary from company to company, a written report to the board discussing activities and actions taken normally is preferable. The committee should use its charter as a guide and supplement the report as needed with minutes of committee meetings. It is best to submit as early as possible, and in writing, any suggestions requiring substantive action by the board, to give board members time to consider and act on proposals.

Other information should go to the board as well. For example, any suggested changes to the committee's charter should be discussed with the board, and its approval obtained, and, as mentioned earlier, the results of evaluations should be communicated.

To Shareholders

For over a decade, a number of organizations—including the Treadway Commission and the Public Oversight Board in the United States—have called for audit committee reporting to shareholders. The objective of these recommendations is to allow shareholders to better understand the audit committee's role in overseeing financial reporting. For various reasons, including fear that reporting might expose committee members to increased liability, few companies have issued such reports.

The SEC has had long-standing rules requiring annual proxy disclosure of the existence and composition of the audit committee, its functions and number of meetings held. Believing that additional disclosures about a company's audit committee and its interaction with auditors and management would promote investor confidence in the integrity of the financial reporting process, the SEC ultimately decided to mandate additional reporting for registrants. Its rules, issued in 1999, require that companies include audit committee reports in their proxy statements. The report must state whether the audit committee:

- Reviewed and discussed the audited financial statements with management
- Discussed with the external auditors the matters required to be discussed by Statement on Auditing Standards No. 61
- Received the written disclosures and letter from the auditors required by Independence Standards Board Standard No. 1 regarding their independence, and discussed the auditors' independence with them
- Based on the above, recommended to the board of directors that the audited financial statements be included in the company's annual report on Form 10-K

It remains to be seen whether non-SEC registrants will issue similar reports of the committee's basic responsibilities and activities, in the hope of achieving better communication.

Other Reports

Depending on jurisdiction, audit committee activity may need to be reported to regulators or others. For example, the NYSE, NASD and AMEX require written confirmation to them on audit committee member qualifications and related board determinations, as well as the review and re-evaluation of the audit committee charter.

CHAPTER 7
MEETINGS

To be positioned to effectively carry out its responsibilities, the audit committee must meet periodically, and hold special meetings as warranted. The right parties need to participate, sometimes in private session, with agendas covering all committee responsibilities and sufficient time for in-depth discussions. While off-line communications are becoming more prevalent and contribute to effectiveness, the audit committee meeting is where most of the action is, and must be well executed for committee success.

Frequency and Duration

How frequently should audit committees meet? The committee's objectives and scope drive the number of meetings, with most committees' meetings coinciding with key steps in the financial reporting and audit cycles.

Our 1993 research showed that audit committees met on average 3.3 times a year, with those considered "state of the art" meeting 4 times. The National Association of Corporate Directors' (NACD) 1999–2000 Public Company Governance Survey shows 47 percent of audit committees now meet at least 4 times annually, with almost one in five scheduling 5 or more meetings.

Looking at results of the COSO study on *Fraudulent Financial Reporting: 1987–1997,* the importance of frequent audit committee meetings is highlighted in the negative. The study found that most of the audit committees of "fraud companies" met only once a year, while some didn't meet at all. Although cause and effect might not be proved, the correlation is telling.

Best practice has meeting frequency tracking audit committee responsibilities. Committees that review quarterly and annual reports before issuance generally meet at least four times each year. Some also meet at year-end to review a draft of the annual financial statements containing preliminary results, if final numbers are not yet available. It considers new accounting and reporting issues, along with statement format and other changes from the prior year, allowing a directed focus on "final" numbers when they become available.

While the meeting schedule often matches the financial reporting cycle, the committee must address its other responsibilities as well. For issues demanding significant discussion, such as reviewing audit plans or dealing with important compliance or risk management issues, one meeting might be extended or a separate one scheduled. Most audit committees have the authority to hold special meetings as circumstances warrant, and the committee's charter should provide for such meetings.

It is vital that committee members be given sufficient time to discuss important matters. While committee meetings typically are scheduled to coincide with board meetings, they should not be so tightly scheduled as to restrict time needed to fully discuss issues. And, there should be flexibility to extend discussion if needed.

How long should meetings last? Too many variables exist to establish a standard or minimum meeting length. Rather, duration should be dictated by the time required to effectively cover the agenda. Our 1993 research showed that, on average, meetings for state-of-the-art audit committees lasted just over two hours. In 2000, the NACD Blue Ribbon Commission on Audit Committees suggested that meetings last half a day. Based on the expanding role of the committee, it's difficult to see how requisite attention to its responsibilities can be adequately given in less time. The practice of convening audit committee meetings for a short period immediately before a board meeting is difficult to justify.

The acid test is whether committee members are satisfied they have thoroughly addressed all significant agenda items, without feeling undue pressure to rush discussions.

Briefing Materials

To enhance effectiveness, briefing materials should be supplied well in advance of meetings, and committee members should take the necessary time to fully prepare. Generally, materials are prepared and distributed by management, and often include special reports from the internal audit director and external auditors on matters they will address at the meeting. Some companies provide information to committee members between meetings, better enabling members to stay on top of issues and trends developing at the company, and providing them a more robust understanding of the results.

Audit committee members initially might think the volume of information they receive is more than sufficient, but they should not necessarily rely solely on information provided by management. Committee members should proactively determine what information they want, and work with management to get it. By determining its needs, the committee can prevent a lack of information or information overload.

Audit committee chairs often play an important role by reviewing draft briefing material and discussing and clarifying issues with management in separate meetings before the committee meeting. This allows the chair to better understand which issues are relevant and ensure the committee obtains what's needed.

Participants

Both the internal audit director and external auditors regularly attend audit committee meetings. Because management is responsible for the financial reporting process, its active participation in committee meetings is important. The CFO and controller commonly attend, and it is not uncommon for the CEO and general counsel to attend at least parts of some meetings. Functional specialists such as the general counsel, tax director, information technology director or corporate secretary attend selected meetings when the agenda calls for their expertise. Our 1993 survey found that in almost 90 percent of companies, management regularly attended audit committee meetings.

While management can provide information helpful to the committee in its deliberations, the committee must remain alert so that management does not, unintentionally or otherwise, divert attention from sensitive matters.

Some audit committees now require that business operations management whose departments have significant control weaknesses or issues attend and report to the committee on how they are addressing the issues. This has many benefits, a key one being that it signals that directors are focusing on significant risk exposures and take them seriously.

Most audit committees do not routinely invite outside specialists to their meetings, except for the external auditors. Those committees that do are likely to invite environmental engineers, pension or actuarial consultants, or legal counsel.

To maximize effectiveness, and support an atmosphere that allows frank discussion of confidential matters, attendance should be limited to those who can make a contribution to agenda topics. Experience shows that a small group does better in getting to the heart of issues and dealing with them effectively. At the same time, other board directors usually are allowed to attend committee meetings, if they choose, to observe or raise issues, and such participation can be very positive. Indeed, some boards avoid scheduling multiple board committee meetings concurrently for this reason.

Private Meetings

The audit committee should meet privately with the internal audit director and the external auditors, and hold private executive sessions to discuss issues such as auditor performance, management's performance, future agenda topics or how the committee might improve its own performance.

As reflected in Exhibit 7.1, our 1999 survey shows that most audit committees hold separate private meetings with the external auditors and internal audit at least annually. Interestingly, although 9 percent of committee chairs said the committee never meets privately with internal audit, 31 percent of internal audit directors said such private meetings never occur. This disparity might be due to a larger number of, and more geographically distributed, internal audit directors responding to this survey question.

Best practice calls for these private sessions to be scheduled as part of the ongoing agenda. While some companies hold such sessions only at the request of the internal audit director or external auditors, the request itself might raise a red flag with management, diminishing confidentiality.

Exhibit 7.1: Private Sessions with the Audit Committee		
Frequency of Executive Sessions	**1993 Survey**	**1999 Survey**
Internal Audit		
All regular meetings	33%	54%
At least once a year	33%	28%
On an ad hoc basis	24%	9%
Never	10%	9%
External Auditor		
All regular meetings	49%	71%
At least once a year	33%	23%
On an ad hoc basis	11%	6%
Never	7%	0%

Source: Audit Committee Chair Survey

The committee might need to actively ensure that meetings are indeed private. The chair of one committee found it necessary to ask an executive to leave the private meeting—in this case, a former board member recruited to head the finance function. The chair of another committee similarly advised the company's CEO that privacy was required.

Agenda

A detailed written agenda, along with briefing materials, should be distributed before each meeting. Well-crafted agendas help keep the committee focused on accomplishing what it needs to in each meeting, and are most effective when the most important topics are listed first.

Management usually drafts the meeting agenda for the committee chair, who should shape it to his or her satisfaction before it is distributed. In some companies, the internal audit director is tasked with drafting the agenda and working with the chair to finalize it, with the objective of ensuring that all relevant issues are included on the committee's radar screen.

To help ensure that the committee fulfills all its duties and responsibilities over the course of a year, many committees develop an annual meeting schedule, identifying how responsibilities are to be distributed across meetings. The schedule is then used as a starting point in developing the agenda for each meeting. The illustrative schedule in Exhibit 7.2 shows some standard responsibilities based on an audit committee that meets four times annually.

Indeed, the Public Oversight Board's Panel on Audit Effectiveness recommended in its 2000 report that audit committees develop this type of formal calendar of activities, including a meeting plan, and that it be reviewed and agreed to by the board.

Exhibit 7.2: Sample Audit Committee Schedule **(December 31 Year-End)**				
	Feb	**May**	**Aug**	**Nov**
Financial and Related Reporting				
Review of financial results for the quarter and/or year	X	X	X	X
Review of draft Form 10-Q/quarterly public filing		X	X	X
Review of draft Form 10-K/annual public filing	X			
Review of proxy materials and narrative reporting	X			
Status of reserves/estimates	(as required)			X
Current accounting and financial reporting matters	X	X	X	X
Planned changes in accounting principles	(as required)			X
Other matters, including required auditors communications	X	X	X	X
Controls and Compliance				
Legal matters	(as required)			X
Tax matters			X	
Information systems		X		
Regulatory matters (as appropriate)	(as required)			X
Internal Audit				
Internal audit charter				X
Internal audit plan		X		
Internal audit budget and staffing		X		
Coordination with external auditors		X		
Internal audit objectivity and independence		X		
Summary of significant findings	X	X	X	X
Compliance with IIA Standards				X
Private session with internal audit director	X	X	X	X
External Auditors				
Appointment of external auditors	X			
External auditors' independence		X		
External auditors' audit plan		X		
External auditors' internal control findings		X		X
Private session with external auditors	X	X	X	X
Other Committee Activities				
Minutes of previous meeting	X	X	X	X
Audit committee charter			X	
Audit committee self-assessment			X	
Report to the board of directors	X	X	X	X
Report to shareholders	X			

CHAPTER 8
THE FUTURE

As stakeholders look to audit committees to further strengthen financial reporting and achieve other corporate governance objectives, committees continue to respond positively. The impetus for improvement comes from legislators, regulators and institutional investors, and the litigious environment, as well as from the board itself.

Our 1993 study presented a view of the future provided to us by others. This time, we predict which emerging issues, forces and trends will shape the audit committee of the future.

Emerging Issues

So what does the future hold? Our crystal ball sees the following.

Risk Management and Internal Control

The conceptualization of risk management already has moved well beyond insurable risks and risks of unreliable financial reporting. Attention has moved toward early identification and management of a wider range of risks, and we expect significantly more focus on managing key risks to achieving companies' business objectives. In the coming years we see not only more commonality in the language and concepts of risk management, but also better design and more widespread integration of risk management architectures in major businesses. Similarly, we anticipate stronger bonding of risk management and internal control models, with benefits to business of greater effectiveness and efficiency.

Boards of directors and in some cases audit committees will see a need to provide oversight, and, indeed, might themselves provide the impetus for expanded risk management. Because of its wide-ranging scope, we believe some boards will delegate to a newly formed committee oversight responsibility for risk management and control beyond financial reporting.

Faster Communication of Information

Already we see increasing demand for faster disclosure of financial and nonfinancial information, and nothing indicates this trend will lessen. In addition to demand, with the use of new technologies—including the Internet—information flows will continue to accelerate. Yes, "fair disclosure" rules and other regulators' initiatives will help ensure a level playing field. But the capital markets will continue to expect more and more information—more quickly disseminated—and companies will find it in their interest to satisfy these appetites. At the same time, reliability of information will continue to be expected, and be crucial, for communications to achieve intended objectives.

We expect increased focus on the systems that develop information, and on management processes that sharpen estimates, cull what should or should not be shared with the outside world, and promote compliance with regulatory disclosure rules. Audit committees will devote increasing attention to these systems, processes and related internal controls, with likely assistance from internal and external auditors. The stakes will be high, and the board and audit committee will want to enable the company to gain competitive advantage while avoiding communications fiascos.

Expanded Information

Recent years have seen calls for significantly expanded information disclosure, from analysts, institutional investors, environmentalists and other stakeholders, using terms like "sustainability," encompassing a long-term view of environmental footprints, and "triple bottom line" reporting—covering social and environmental results as well as financial. While different, with some information focusing primarily inward and some outward, much of this reporting seeks to communicate corporate achievement far beyond the financial realm. Some of the calls for more information speak to "transparency," wanting to look behind published financial reports and into what's "really" going on in the company. And, with capital markets clearly valuing companies very differently than is accomplished with historically based financial statements, there will be added focus on new accounting and reporting models that provide meaningful valuations encompassing intangibles like intellectual capital, brand equity, research and development, customer base, and the like.

We have little doubt that these new models will take shape and have increasing relevance in the marketplace and with stakeholders, and that boards will find it essential to closely monitor and help shape the new processes. We feel certain that boards naturally will look to the audit committee as best equipped to provide the required oversight to make these communication modes well controlled and reliable.

Reliance on Others

As the committee's scope continues to expand, something has to change. Audit committee members, already stretched thin, will find it virtually impossible to perform effectively without changing the way they operate and looking to additional resources. It seems no responsibilities are taken away, and, indeed, even without new ones, the complexity of the environment and most companies' activities continue to make the job more demanding. If even some of the responsibilities discussed here are added, demand for time and energy could become intolerable.

We expect audit committees to look increasingly to the internal audit director, chief compliance office, chief risk officer, external auditors and others for help in carrying out their responsibilities. Certainly, we see audit committees expanding the number or duration of meetings, and increasingly taking advantage of technology—video conferencing, Intranets, and the like—to communicate. But that won't be enough. New models are likely. Going forward, we expect to see audit committees establishing working groups, composed of nonboard-level individuals with the requisite knowledge and independence, to deal with specific issues and report back to the committee.

Liability

There long have been concerns, especially in litigious environments, about director liability, and recent events such as the new listing and Securities and Exchange Commission (SEC) rules in the United States have exacerbated those concerns. These may play out in departures from audit committees or greater difficulty recruiting qualified new members, in the belief that audit committee members may face more liability than other board members.

Additionally, as responsibilities further increase and expectations rise, we might expect to see more refusals of requests for audit committee service. Should a prominent legal case hold audit committee members liable, it will be a safe bet that quality individuals will think at least twice before remaining on or joining audit committees. The availability and comprehensiveness of director and officer insurance coverage ultimately might be the deciding factor.

More Time, More Pay

Clearly, board and committee service carries many rewards, including professional, emotional, social and financial. Some directors might serve without financial remuneration, but many would not.

With expanding responsibilities and time commitments, boards will need to decide on compensation that is fair and adequate to recruit and retain high-quality directors. We believe compensation in varying forms will increase accordingly, and we believe appropriately.

Issues from Our 1993 Report

A few elements identified in our 1993 report continue to have relevance for the audit committee of the future.

International Operations

Business operations and capital formation were becoming increasingly international in 1993, with foreign acquisitions and currency transactions proliferating. Accounting principles varied by country, with signs that international standards might be forthcoming. Our 1993 report indicated that these areas would require increased audit committee attention.

Today, we see that those trends have continued unabated, with "globalization" the watchword. In addition to increasingly global operations and transactions, we've witnessed convergence of industries on a global basis. And the international accounting standard setters have gained structure and stature.

Looking forward, there is little doubt these patterns will continue, and they may well accelerate. Audit committees of the future will need even better knowledge of company operations, including newly conceived and globally integrated supply chains, production processes, and marketing and sales channels, to allow them to deal with related internal control and financial reporting implications. And, as international accounting standards move toward acceptability, committees will need to understand and deal with them, initially together with, and perhaps ultimately in place of, current national standards. Those committees that monitor compliance matters also will have to be cognizant of the changing legal environment in areas of foreign operations—as environmental regulations and workplace standards continue to evolve, based partly on international pressure.

Joint Ventures and Partnerships

Our 1993 report predicted joint ventures and partnerships would become more financially significant, as companies continued their search for competitive advantage, with audit committees needing to extend their oversight to those enterprises.

It's now clear that the ensuing years saw exactly that, as companies seized opportunities to share expertise, technology and investment in achieving new strategic imperatives. And audit committees indeed have struggled to deal with the issues and financial reporting of ventures where control is less than complete.

Looking ahead, we see companies continuing to deal with global competition and emerging opportunities through joint ventures, alliances, partnerships and other new relationships. The transactions will become more complex, with cycle times shrinking further. Audit committees not only will need to cope with the accelerated pace, but also might be expected by the board to oversee due diligence in the negotiation stage and then post-close to look at the ventures' financial reporting processes and controls. And committees will have to cope with fundamental paradigm shift, as companies form alliances—perhaps driven by e-business opportunities—with competitors, bringing new challenges to oversight.

Training Audit Committee Members

Our 1993 report anticipated that with audit committees' enlarged roles, committee members would be more focused on keeping current with additional information and training. As audit committees' responsibilities have been looked at increasingly by regulators and others, and expanded, committee members have called for and received more training.

It's clear, however, that many committee members are not receiving enough training. Going forward, we believe committees will recruit more technically proficient members, and members will have more internal briefings on technical and business issues and attend more external programs. Nevertheless, we believe that due to the rapidly expanding complexity of the business environment and financial reporting, audit committees are not likely to stay current, and might even fall further behind.

Monitoring Management Estimates

The significance of estimates in financial statements was seen in 1993, with provisions for restructuring and other nonrecurring items becoming commonplace, and emerging accounting requirements—such as those relating to postretirement benefits—requiring more in-depth audit committee attention.

Certainly that trend has continued, with estimates becoming increasingly important to financial reporting in areas including health care benefits, asset impairment, derivatives and revenue recognition. We've seen the SEC in the United States pressing financial statement preparers, auditors and audit committees to play a greater role in preventing manipulation of estimated amounts for "earnings management."

As business transactions become even more complex and financial reporting models shift focus toward more accurate reporting of values, we expect to see even greater and more sophisticated use of estimates. There is little doubt that audit committees will need to understand the new analytic methods and reporting models and how estimates play into them.

Reporting on Internal Control

Our 1993 study pointed to increasing demand to report on the adequacy of internal control over financial and nonfinancial systems, noting that there were few requirements to report publicly— banking in the United States being an exception—and limited voluntary reporting. We noted that as public reporting became more widespread, audit committees would need to be involved in oversight.

Despite continued recommendations, and while companies in some countries report on *responsibility* for internal control and for conducting control assessments, no progress has occurred on positive reporting on internal control *effectiveness*. With increasing analyst and investor demand for up-to-the-minute data, we expect growing demand for information reliability. And with capital markets often moving as much on release of nonfinancial information as financial, systems and controls contributing to the reliability of all types of information increasingly will be subjected to scrutiny. Accordingly, we expect continued pressure for public reporting, and, with it, audit committees will need to keep pace with their oversight.

Information Technology

The growing importance of computer systems and controls was highlighted in 1993, with the anticipation of greater decentralization through networks, and access by customers and suppliers via electronic data interchange. In fact, the rate and extent of change have been greater than almost anyone might have anticipated, with interconnectivity, portability, power and speed expanding exponentially. In addition, e-business has emerged—reshaping business strategies and providing entirely new ways of doing business.

Audit committees are struggling to catch up to, or at least not fall further behind, the curve. The job has become much more difficult, and we expect demands on committee members to continue to expand. And the issues aren't simply reporting or accounting—they involve company survival, resiliency and success.

Interim Reporting

In 1993, we pointed to recommendations from the Macdonald Commission in Canada and the Cadbury Committee in the United Kingdom that audit committees review interim reports, and predicted more prefiling committee involvement. Since then there has been significantly more committee focus on interim reporting, with the majority of committees outside the United States embracing such involvement. But similar attention by committees of U.S. companies has lagged.

With new requirements in the United States for external auditor review of interim financial results and communicating related information to the audit committee, we look for increasing committee involvement. Although there is no requirement for the audit committee to review the interim reports, we expect that the required auditor involvement and communications to the audit committee, coupled with greater market focus, will drive this attention.

Compliance with Laws and Regulations and Codes of Conduct

Based on the issuance of the Federal Sentencing Guidelines in the United States in 1991, our 1993 report predicted more board and audit committee attention to compliance programs. Since then, with the influential Caremark decision, there has been greater attention to this area, with boards delegating often significant oversight responsibility to the audit committee.

With the presumption that human nature will remain what it is, together with the complexity of legislation and the litigious nature of society, compliance programs will continue to require ongoing attention by audit committees.

APPENDIX A
SELF-ASSESSMENT GUIDE

The following Guide summarizes key principles and practices discussed in this report, and is provided for your use in assessing your audit committee's performance. You may find it useful to rate the extent to which your committee complies with each statement, on a scale where 1 = Strongly Disagree and 5 = Strongly Agree. If the practice is not being followed or if the rating is below what you consider acceptable, space is provided to note steps your committee should take to raise performance. You also might want to use that column to capture any personal actions you wish to take.

PRINCIPAL COMPONENTS OF EFFECTIVE AUDIT COMMITTEES	Board Rating (1-5)	FOLLOW-UP ACTIONS (Including any personal plans)
Financial Statements **Your committee:** Is satisfied the company adequately **addresses the risk** that the financial statements may be **materially misstated**, intentionally or unintentionally		
Is comfortable, through **discussions with management and external auditors**, that accounting principles followed by the company and any **changes** in accounting principles are **appropriate**		
Thoroughly **reviews** the **reasons for** any **changes** in **accounting principles** made at management's **discretion**, understanding potential regulator and market reaction, before granting approval		

PRINCIPAL COMPONENTS OF EFFECTIVE AUDIT COMMITTEES	Board Rating (1-5)	FOLLOW-UP ACTIONS (Including any personal plans)
Scrutinizes areas involving **management judgment**—significant accounting accruals, reserves or other **estimates**—that have a **material impact** on the **financial statements**		
Discusses with management reasons for all **significant variances** in the financial statements **between years** and **from budget**, ensuring the **explanations** are **consistent with** members' understanding of the **business**		
Thoroughly discusses with management **unusual or complex** items and their **accounting treatment**, ensuring **consistency with knowledge** of company		
Reviews **narrative reporting** and other information included in reports to ensure they **are supportable** by information in the financial statements or other information known to members		
Discusses with management, the external auditors and the internal audit director any **significant accounting and reporting issues** during the period and **concurs** with their **resolution**		

PRINCIPAL COMPONENTS OF EFFECTIVE AUDIT COMMITTEES	Board Rating (1-5)	FOLLOW-UP ACTIONS (Including any personal plans)
Discusses **audit results** with the **external auditors** and considers management's handling of proposed **audit adjustments**		
Meets periodically with **general counsel** and outside counsel to discuss **legal matters** having **significant impact** on the financial statements		
Discusses with management and external auditors the **substance of any significant issues** raised by counsel **concerning litigation, contingencies, claims or assessments**, understanding their **impact** on the financial statements		
Assesses the **financial statements as a whole** for completeness and consistency with information known to members, discussing also with management and the external auditors		
Oversees the **interim reporting** process, reviewing and discussing interim financial reports before they are filed with regulators		

PRINCIPAL COMPONENTS OF EFFECTIVE AUDIT COMMITTEES	Board Rating (1-5)	FOLLOW-UP ACTIONS (Including any personal plans)
Risk, Control, Compliance **Your committee:** Clearly **understands** and agrees with the board on **which elements of internal control**—financial reporting, operational effectiveness and efficiency, and compliance with laws and regulations—**it oversees** on behalf of the board		
Reviews the **extent of control testing by** internal and external **auditors**, understanding the **degree to which it can be relied on** to detect internal control problems or fraud		
Discusses with internal and external **auditors** their observations on **internal control** effectiveness and **any significant weaknesses** or issues **found**		
Sees that management **addresses**, on a timely basis, significant **control exposures**, relying on internal and external auditors as required to **assess adequacy** of corrective actions taken		

PRINCIPAL COMPONENTS OF EFFECTIVE AUDIT COMMITTEES	Board Rating (1-5)	FOLLOW-UP ACTIONS (Including any personal plans)
Monitors company **compliance with laws and regulations** in areas in which it has oversight responsibility, **through periodic briefings** from internal audit, general counsel, compliance officer and management, among others		
Reviews periodically the program management established to **communicate** the company's **code of conduct** and **monitor** compliance, understanding **systemic issues** and management's plans to address them		
Retains the **authority** to conduct **special investigations**, doing so and **engaging outside resources** to assist, as appropriate		
Is **comfortable** with the nature and extent of **responsibilities delegated** to the committee **by** the **board**, and has **sufficient time** and resources to carry them out effectively		
Interaction with Management, Auditors **Your committee:** Maintains a **productive relationship with management**, with open lines of communication and **ongoing dialogue**		

PRINCIPAL COMPONENTS OF EFFECTIVE AUDIT COMMITTEES	Board Rating (1-5)	FOLLOW-UP ACTIONS (Including any personal plans)
Meets periodicallys in **executive session** to assess **management's effectiveness**		
Absent an established **internal audit function**, periodically **revisits** with management the **need to establish** such a function in the company		
Reviews and **approves internal audit's charter**, also ensuring the function **reports** to an appropriately **senior position** within the company, maintaining internal audit's **objectivity**		
Reviews and **concurs in** the appointment, replacement or dismissal of the **internal audit director, ensuring** internal audit's continued **objectivity**		
Reviews internal audit plans, **ensuring appropriate internal audit coverage** of key control systems, and proper degree of coordination of work with external auditors		

PRINCIPAL COMPONENTS OF EFFECTIVE AUDIT COMMITTEES	Board Rating (1-5)	FOLLOW-UP ACTIONS (Including any personal plans)
Reviews the **adequacy** of **internal audit staffing** and **budget**, focusing on **staff quality** and **continuity**, as well as the impact of any outsourcing		
Discusses **significant** internal **audit findings**, reported to the committee in **appropriate detail**, as well as the **status** of **past** audit **recommendations**		
Is satisfied through discussions with management and auditors that **internal audit** is **operationally independent** of the areas it assesses, and by its support, assists in preserving such independence		
Inquires whether **internal audit** activities **comply** with The Institute of Internal Auditors' *Standards for the Professional Practice of Internal Auditing*		
Accepts ultimate authority for selection or reappointment of the **external auditors**, considering management input and its own observations on firm quality, and ensures any recommendation for dismissal is for **appropriate reasons**		

PRINCIPAL COMPONENTS OF EFFECTIVE AUDIT COMMITTEES	Board Rating (1-5)	FOLLOW-UP ACTIONS (Including any personal plans)
Ensures **external auditors' independence**, receiving and discussing reports on the **extent of nonaudit services** and **other relationships** that could bear on independence, and related safeguards		
Reviews the **external audit scope** and related **fees**, ensuring members understand and are **comfortable with** the **extent** of audit **work** anticipated		
Receives **information** required to be communicated under **auditing standards**, covering such matters as significant **accounting principles** and the auditors' judgment about their quality, audit **adjustments, major issues** encountered, **fraud** and **illegal acts**, and **significant deficiencies** in **internal control**		
Is satisfied that **engagement of any audit firm** other than the principal authors is based on **sound rationale**		
Is **familiar** with situations in which **management seeks a second opinion** on significant accounting or auditing issues		

PRINCIPAL COMPONENTS OF EFFECTIVE AUDIT COMMITTEES	Board Rating (1-5)	FOLLOW-UP ACTIONS (Including any personal plans)
Instructs both the internal and external **auditors** that the **committee expects** to be **advised** of any areas requiring its attention		
Builds constructive **professional relationships with** both internal and external **auditors**, facilitating their ease at **bringing forward sensitive issues**		
Meets **privately** with both internal and external **auditors** on a **routine basis**; such meetings are not dependent on a special request		
Creates an **atmosphere of trust**, encouraging candid discussions with all parties		
Committee Composition **Your committee:** Has its **new members selected** by designated **independent directors, identifying needed skills/attributes**		

PRINCIPAL COMPONENTS OF EFFECTIVE AUDIT COMMITTEES	Board Rating (1-5)	FOLLOW-UP ACTIONS (Including any personal plans)
Members possess characteristics such as integrity, judgment, credibility, trustworthiness, intuition, industry knowledge, willingness to actively participate, ability to constructively handle conflict, and communication, decision-making and interpersonal skills		
Members possess requisite level of **financial reporting knowledge**, or acquire such knowledge soon after joining the committee, ensuring any applicable rules are met		
Members all are **independent**, according to applicable regulatory/stock exchange definitions and requirements set by the board		
Is satisfied it has a **sufficiently independent** voice, in no way beholden to the chief executive, and is **consistently ready** to **constructively challenge** the management team		
Considers, with the board, a need for **balancing continuity** with **fresh perspective** when considering members' **terms** of service		

PRINCIPAL COMPONENTS OF EFFECTIVE AUDIT COMMITTEES	Board Rating (1-5)	FOLLOW-UP ACTIONS (Including any personal plans)
Is the **right size**, bringing requisite knowledge, abilities and skills to the table in a **group small enough** to **act cohesively**		
Training and Resources **Your committee:** Ensures **new members** have the **robust orientation** required to understand the committee's **responsibilities** and the **financial reporting process** they will oversee		
Sees that all members are provided **continuing information** and **training** on **business** and **accounting developments**		
Is comfortable that management and auditor **briefings**, independent member **reading** and **formal training sessions** combine to **provide** all **required development** members need to be effective		
Makes sure it commands **adequate resources** to support it in accomplishing its objectives		

PRINCIPAL COMPONENTS OF EFFECTIVE AUDIT COMMITTEES	Board Rating (1-5)	FOLLOW-UP ACTIONS (Including any personal plans)
Charter, Evaluation, Reporting **Your committee:** Operates pursuant to a **written charter** that has been **approved** by the **board of directors**		
Charter **clearly articulates** the committee's: • **Purpose** • **Responsibilities** • **Composition** • **Authority** • **Reporting responsibilities**		
Assesses its charter annually, suggesting required **updates** to the board for its approval		
Ensures annually that it has **carried out all** the **responsibilities** outlined in its charter		
Is satisfied that it is properly **positioned** to **comply** with any **new rules** or **requirements**		

PRINCIPAL COMPONENTS OF EFFECTIVE AUDIT COMMITTEES	Board Rating (1-5)	FOLLOW-UP ACTIONS (Including any personal plans)
Regularly evaluates performance of the **committee as** a **whole**, and takes decisive corrective action		
Regularly evaluates individual members' performance, and takes decisive corrective action		
Operates in an **atmosphere** of **openness** and **trust**, where members feel **free** to **speak their minds** and **pursue issues to conclusion**		
Reports regularly on its **activities**, key **issues** and **major recommendations** to the board of directors		
Provides reports to **shareholders**, on committee responsibilities and other matters, as the committee deems appropriate or is required by rule		

PRINCIPAL COMPONENTS OF EFFECTIVE AUDIT COMMITTEES	Board Rating (1-5)	FOLLOW-UP ACTIONS (Including any personal plans)
Meetings **Your committee:** Holds **sufficient number** of meetings, **scheduled at appropriate points** to address its responsibilities on a timely basis		
Meetings are of **adequate length** to allow the committee to accomplish its agenda, with **time** to **fully discuss** issues		
Meetings are effective, with **advance buy-in on** the **agenda**, and the **right amount** of quality **advance material distributed** in a **timely** manner, which members review before meetings		
Makes sure the **right individuals** attend, particularly those with **meaningful input** on agenda items		
Members **regularly meet in private sessions** with both the **internal** audit director and **external auditors**, to allow **full** and **frank discussion** of potentially sensitive matters		

PRINCIPAL COMPONENTS OF EFFECTIVE AUDIT COMMITTEES	Board Rating (1-5)	FOLLOW-UP ACTIONS (Including any personal plans)
Members **regularly** meet in **executive session**, allowing **confidential discussion** of financial reporting reliability and auditor and management performance		
The Future **Your committee:** Considers whether there are **emerging issues** that will demand its attention going forward, and is **proactive** in positioning itself to deal with them		

APPENDIX B
SAMPLE AUDIT
COMMITTEE CHARTER

The following sample charter captures many of the best practices outlined in this report. Of course, no sample charter encompasses all activities that might be appropriate to a particular audit committee, nor will all activities identified in a sample charter be relevant to every committee. Accordingly, this charter must be tailored to each committee's needs and governing rules.

Audit Committee Charter

Purpose

To assist the board of directors in fulfilling its oversight responsibilities for the financial reporting process, the system of internal control over financial reporting, the audit process, and the company's process for monitoring compliance with laws and regulations and the code of conduct.

Authority

The audit committee has authority to conduct or authorize investigations into any matters within its scope of responsibility. It is empowered to:
- Retain outside counsel, accountants or others to advise the committee or assist in the conduct of an investigation
- Seek any information it requires from employees—all of whom are directed to cooperate with the committee's requests—or external parties
- Meet with company officers, external auditors or outside counsel, as necessary

Composition

The audit committee will consist of at least three and no more than six members of the board of directors. The board or its nominating committee will appoint committee members and the committee chair.

Each committee member will be both independent and financially literate, as defined by applicable regulation and the board of directors. At least one member shall have expertise in financial reporting.

Meetings

The committee will meet at least four times a year, with authority to convene additional meetings, as circumstances require. All committee members are expected to attend each meeting, in person or via tele- or video-conference. The committee will invite members of management, auditors or others to attend meetings and provide pertinent information, as necessary. It will hold private meetings with auditors (see below) and executive sessions. Meeting agendas will be prepared and provided in advance to members, along with appropriate briefing materials. Minutes will be prepared.

Responsibilities

The committee will carry out the following responsibilities:

Financial Statements

- Review significant accounting and reporting issues, including complex or unusual transactions and highly judgmental areas, and recent professional and regulatory pronouncements, and understand their impact on the financial statements
- Review with management and the external auditors the results of the audit, including any difficulties encountered
- Review the annual financial statements, and consider whether they are complete, consistent with information known to committee members, and reflect appropriate accounting principles
- Review other sections of the annual report and related regulatory filings before release and consider the accuracy and completeness of the information
- Review with management and the external auditors all matters required to be communicated to the committee under generally accepted auditing standards
- Understand how management develops interim financial information, and the nature and extent of internal and external auditor involvement
- Review interim financial reports with management and the external auditors, before filing with regulators, and consider whether they are complete and consistent with the information known to committee members

Internal Control

- Consider the effectiveness of the company's internal control over annual and interim financial reporting, including information technology security and control
- Understand the scope of internal and external auditors' review of internal control over financial reporting, and obtain reports on significant findings and recommendations, together with management's responses

Internal Audit

- Review with management and the internal audit director the charter, plans, activities, staffing and organizational structure of the internal audit function
- Ensure there are no unjustified restrictions or limitations, and review and concur in the appointment, replacement or dismissal of the internal audit director
- Review the effectiveness of the internal audit function, including compliance with The Institute of Internal Auditors' *Standards for the Professional Practice of Internal Auditing*
- On a regular basis, meet separately with the director of internal audit to discuss any matters that the committee or internal audit believes should be discussed privately

External Audit

- Review the external auditors' proposed audit scope and approach, including coordination of audit effort with internal audit
- Review the performance of the external auditors, and exercise final approval on the appointment or discharge of the auditors
- Review and confirm the independence of the external auditors by obtaining statements from the auditors on relationships between the auditors and the company, including nonaudit services, and discussing the relationships with the auditors
- On a regular basis, meet separately with the external auditors to discuss any matters that the committee or auditors believe should be discussed privately

Compliance

- Review the effectiveness of the system for monitoring compliance with laws and regulations and the results of management's investigation and follow-up (including disciplinary action) of any instances of noncompliance
- Review the findings of any examinations by regulatory agencies, and any auditor observations
- Review the process for communicating the code of conduct to company personnel, and for monitoring compliance therewith
- Obtain regular updates from management and company legal counsel regarding compliance matters

Reporting Responsibilities

- Regularly report to the board of directors about committee activities, issues and related recommendations
- Provide an open avenue of communication between internal audit, the external auditors and the board of directors
- Report annually to the shareholders, describing the committee's composition, responsibilities and how they were discharged, and any other information required by rule
- Review any other reports the company issues that relate to committee responsibilities

Other Responsibilities

- Perform other activities related to this charter as requested by the board of directors
- Institute and oversee special investigations as needed
- Review and assess the adequacy of the committee charter annually, requesting board approval for proposed changes
- Confirm annually that all responsibilities outlined in this charter have been carried out
- Evaluate the committee's and individual members' performance on a regular basis

APPENDIX C
E-BUSINESS

Internet-based and other information technologies are transforming critical business functions and converging under a new name—e-business—to dramatically change the way companies do business. This was borne out in the findings of a 1999 survey of over 800 CEOs of global companies, sponsored jointly by PricewaterhouseCoopers and the World Economic Forum. CEOs predict formidable new competition in their industries and significant new revenue growth through e-business, with half of all respondents saying competitors using e-business as a main channel to their customers are likely to pose a significant threat.

What Is E-Business?

E-business encompasses e-commerce (performing business transactions using Internet technology), e-content (publishing content on Internet web sites), and e-collaboration (sharing data and applications between Internet-based tools and users).

E-business also can be looked at in terms of types of transactions:

- *Business-to-consumer*, including marketing and selling products, handling and filling orders, and electronic payment
- *Business-to-business*, divided into "buy side," such as procurement applications designed to automate corporate purchasing, and "sell side," such as catalogue-based applications allowing high-volume customers to configure and price orders
- *Multiple suppliers and buyers* ("the electronic marketplace"), bringing together suppliers and buyers, and providing trading functionality for transacting business, such as online auctions, barter and "communities"

Electronic data interchange (EDI), a well established but very expensive type of e-business, is being superseded, and the whole range of business-to-business applications extended, by the Internet. For example, major auto manufacturers increasingly are running their supplier networks via the World Wide Web.

Impacts of E-Business

E-business is transforming businesses and industries to varying extents as they use the Internet in pursuing the following goals:

- *Channel enhancement*—enhancing brands, attracting new customers, selling globally at no increased cost, providing 24-hour service, automating targeted promotions and increasing customer convenience
- *Value chain integration*—linking with suppliers/retailers/distributors, propagating orders in real time, reducing inventory levels, sharing information and eliminating wholesalers and retailers that do not add value
- *Industry transformation*—fundamentally changing the way industries operate, a notable example being the music industry where the possibility now exists for artists to publish music on the Web, bypassing publishers, wholesalers and retailers
- *Convergence*—offering products/services outside the organization's traditional area of expertise, such as supermarkets offering bank accounts

Managing the Risks

The road to e-business success is not without potholes. The complexity, challenge and change brought about by e-business create risks. Effectively managing these risks will, in many cases, have a major impact on achieving business objectives and enhancing shareholder value. Management must understand the various risks and review the company's risk management policies and practices.

To manage e-business risks effectively, organizations need to consider three primary risk areas: hazard, uncertainty and opportunity.

Hazards

In the e-business arena, significant hazards to consider include:

- *Security.* Traditional theft and fraud are migrating from the paper-based world to the electronic one. Not surprisingly, Internet crime in the United States is estimated to have jumped by 600% during 1999. Organizations must put effective security procedures in place and ensure they remain effective by periodically carrying out penetration testing. Mergers and acquisitions will fuel the need to double check security measures in place. Moreover, as firms establish similar informational and transactional networks involving an expanded range of individuals, additional security measures will be needed.
  Some organizations, in the excitement to get an Internet site up and running and remain competitive, haven't established necessary security procedures. Going forward, management will be forced to recognize areas of security weakness and address them head-on. And, firms will take a more holistic approach to security by building and integrating fail-safes into their e-business systems.

- *Privacy.* Privacy is perceived as a fundamental right, and customers have high expectations that privacy measures will be a top priority of those conducting e-business. A recent PricewaterhouseCoopers survey shows almost 90 percent of users are concerned about privacy measures and nearly 60 percent are very concerned. Privacy protection will become a core component of the e-business infrastructure.
- *E-business resilience.* Customers and business partners expect e-business to be available and highly reliable 24 hours a day, seven days a week. Operational failures can have major consequences.
- *Legal and regulatory issues.* The potential hazards of inappropriate content on a web site can be significant, and once transaction processing is involved, these risks are magnified. The legal framework for digital transactions remains in a state of flux, leaving the legality of certain contracts, signatures and commitments questionable. Civil litigation undoubtedly will be brought against companies failing to adequately protect sensitive data and those who violate e-business privacy. Because e-business transcends geographic boundaries, those engaged in it must understand differing restrictions that prevail in other countries.
- *Taxation.* E-business poses a number of potential taxation hazards, both direct and indirect. For example, locating web servers in a territory for operational reasons may inadvertently create an undesirable tax presence.

Uncertainty

Managing uncertainty involves planning, decision making, implementation and monitoring to ensure day-to-day operations deliver the expected results effectively and efficiently. In the e-business arena, uncertainties include:

- *The change process.* Managing risk inherent in the change process itself is key. This includes putting the right project management processes, structures and skills in place; establishing the right culture through the signals that senior management gives the team; and ensuring all parts of the organization are aligned.
- *Consumer confidence.* A key obstacle to successful e-business is the lack of consumer confidence regarding security, privacy and disclosure of relevant business practices. Programs are being developed to help companies manage this uncertainty by providing relevant information to customers about such matters as sales terms, privacy, security and complaint resolution.
- *Advertiser relationships.* Internet advertising is becoming increasingly important to ensure that targeted customers reach a web site. As advertising spending on the Internet grows, advertisers increasingly will want independently verified pre-buy audience and traffic statistics, to feel confident they are spending their money wisely.

Opportunity

Harnessing the power of risk by exploiting opportunities in the marketplace can create a competitive advantage and increase shareholder value. In the e-business arena, opportunities to consider include:

- *Building customer loyalty.* For example, companies have developed web-based customer self-service tools that provide online access to order processing, billing and customer support applications, resulting in increased customer satisfaction.
- *Optimizing business processes.* For example, some organizations have simplified and streamlined purchasing processes through greater automation, delegation and business rules-based procurement, saving millions of dollars a year.
- *Creating new products and services.* With the right tools, enterprises can create products and services that are completely new—such as online stock trading—or previously were uneconomical to provide. E-business infrastructures also favor fast time to market and flexibility.

Accounting and E-Business

The explosion of e-business, particularly "dot-com" companies, is focusing the accounting profession and regulators on areas where quality financial reporting may be undermined. In the Internet/dot-com world, financial statement users pay significant attention to revenue growth and gross profit margins, often giving less weight to traditional measures of financial performance, like net income. Revenues have been overstated by incorrectly "grossing up" the effect of transactions in which revenues and expenses are reported in offsetting amounts. Other errors result from incorrectly classifying income statement items, such as reporting what are costs of sales as marketing expense, thereby overstating gross profit margins. The notion that such practices, since they do not affect the "bottom line," are subject to different materiality standards is inappropriate.

Then there is the Internet-enabled, warp-speed dissemination of financial and operating information. Information can be filed with regulators electronically, becoming available over the Internet. Additional information and analyses put out by companies or others find their way onto electronic bulletin boards, into chat rooms and elsewhere. With increasing expectations and demand in the marketplace for more readily available input, the environment is moving toward monthly and even more frequent dissemination of data.

There is little formal regulatory process over much of this information. Companies are concerned about information accuracy and consistency with formal reports and filings, and the ability of outsiders to disseminate inaccurate information about corporate results.

Summing It Up

The Internet and other information technologies are dramatically changing how virtually all companies—not just well publicized dot-coms—do business internally and with customers and suppliers. The complexity and challenge brought by e-business create risks as well as opportunities. The risks include hazards to security and privacy, rapidly evolving legal, regulatory and tax structures, impacts on internal control, and financial reporting considerations such as revenue recognition. Audit committees can play a key role in overseeing how the company manages its e-business. This should encompass understanding the nature and ongoing evolution of e-business activities and reviewing risk assessment and business processes intended to ensure e-business activities are implemented and conducted in an effective and controlled manner. Companies need to be aware of the following as being key to successfully managing the risks of e-business, and in fulfilling their oversight responsibilities audit committees will want to consider the extent to which management:

- Has clearly identified how e-business objectives link to critical business issues before starting a project.
- Avoids the trap of treating e-business as just a "front-end" and recognizes that it changes the way the company operates.
- Recognizes that e-business must be a business-driven, not an information technology, initiative.
- Forms a skilled e-business team combining both business and information technology.
- Identifies and encourages senior business champions committed to the project.
- Balances unit ownership with central leadership, coordination and development.
- Plans thoroughly how to integrate e-business into existing business systems.
- Understands the legal and security requirements of e-business.
- Pays attention to culture and change, which are even more challenging than technology.
- Includes key business partners in the company's e-business initiative.
- Has reviewed the appropriateness of accounting and dissemination practices and related internal controls for Internet/dot-com activities.

Audit committees looking to consider e-business issues further may use the accompanying checklist.

Checklist: E-Business — Points of Focus for Audit Committees

Economics of the e-business model

E-Business requires increased focus on viability. New types of business models can make it difficult to assess:

- Unique considerations for e-business start-ups and growth phase companies
- Complex going concern considerations—sustainability of service, customers disappearing quicker than they were generated, never-made-a-profit companies betting on future revenue streams
- More complex impairment considerations (goodwill, capitalized R&D, fixed assets)

Translating the e-business model into results

- Understand how processes are established to deliver the e-business model
- Discuss with technology leaders how technology is delivering the e-business plan
- Understand how the e-business model translates into reported results

Contracts

- Variable terms of trade possible
- What constitutes a contract in an electronic environment
- How management controls contractual risk and administers contracts
- What constitutes reliable documentation/evidence for legal/tax purposes
- Accounting and reporting implications of contractual relationships and terms
- Complex contractual arrangements required to be unbundled for accounting purposes

Outsourcing and alliances

E-business can result in increased reliance on outsourcing, other service providers and alliances.

- Business not confined to legal entities—impact on controls and accounting
- Dependence on contracts to determine operating results

Tax and legal issues

- Tax, regulatory or legal exposures due to unique business models not yet challenged by the taxing, regulatory and legal authorities
- Legal enforceability of electronic documents (electronic contracts, signatures, etc.) that varies by geography and is evolving
- Privacy in sharing customer data (web activity, personal profiles, etc.), including impact of varying data protection laws in different jurisdictions

Checklist: E-Business — Points of Focus for Audit Committees (Cont.)

Increased reliance on controls

Most e-businesses are based on automated and/or high-volume transactions. This means they need processes to get things right the first time, which in turn means increased reliance on process design and operation of preventive controls.

- Significant controls over e-business transactions
- Auditors' assessments of controls over e-business activities and reliance thereon
- Traditional audit approaches may not be practicable because of changes in the way processes are controlled and difficulty obtaining direct evidence for transactions

Accounting issues

Many accounting issues relating to e-business practices are fundamental to the way the market values companies.

- New business models that complicate revenue and cost recognition
- Gross vs. net presentation of transactions or revenue streams, and determining on which line to report costs
- Increasing use of barter, cash floats and free services to customers
- Distinguishing between commitments and liabilities
- Distinguishing between principal and agent when value chain is disaggregated
- Faster, more widespread and less controlled dissemination of company information

APPENDIX D
PROJECT METHOD

This report is based on a review of audit committee literature, surveys, interviews and the knowledge and experience of PricewaterhouseCoopers' professionals.

Literature Search

The project team reviewed literature on audit committees in major developed countries. This included recommendations and guidelines issued by national and international organizations (e.g., stock exchanges, legal associations, regulators), surveys on board and audit committee practices published by organizations such as the National Association of Corporate Directors and the American Society of Corporate Secretaries, and other business publications. Some of the most informative sources drawn on for this report are listed in Appendix E.

Surveys

We surveyed 126 public companies, judgmentally selected across diverse industries from nine countries: Australia, Canada, France, Hong Kong, The Netherlands, New Zealand, Singapore, the United Kingdom and the United States. For the companies selected, the audit committee chair and the internal audit director were identified. In total, 239 questionnaires were distributed, as not every company had an audit committee or an internal audit function.

The audit committee chair survey focused particularly on involvement relative to:

- Roles and responsibilities undertaken by the committee
- Extent of committee interaction with internal and external auditors
- Degree of satisfaction with information, training and other support the committee receives to allow it to effectively discharge its duties

The internal audit director survey focused on:

- Relationship with the audit committee, including extent of committee review of internal audit department matters
- Extent and nature of communications between internal audit and the committee
- Scope of internal audit's work

Thirty-five audit committee chairs (or 30 percent) returned completed surveys, as did 59 internal audit directors (or 48 percent). We gratefully acknowledge these individuals and thank them for the time, effort and care with which they provided their information.

Interview Activities

In conjunction with the research conducted for *Corporate Governance and the Board — What Works Best*, we conducted interviews with 27 directors and corporate governance thought leaders. Many of those individuals are audit committee members or otherwise have insight into effective committee performance, and we used the information gained in the interviews in this report. A complete listing of their names is included in the companion report. We also interviewed 15 internal audit directors. Interview guides were used as a starting point, with the interviewee providing whatever information he or she deemed pertinent. We acknowledge and greatly appreciate all of these individuals who gave their time and shared their experiences, expertise, views and perspectives. Of course, the views expressed in this report are those of PricewaterhouseCoopers.

The internal audit directors interviewed are:

- Bobby W. Alexander, Exxon Corporation
- Fiona Bennett, The Broken Hill Proprietary Company Limited
- LeRoy Bookal, Texaco, Inc.
- Nigel Dean, Coles Myer Ltd.
- Stephen A. Doherty, Credit Lyonnais Americas
- Michel Guenard, Groupe Danone
- Jeanette E. Hughes, Royal & SunAlliance Insurance Group plc
- Howard J. Johnson, J.C. Penney Company, Inc.
- William M. McDonough, Jr., Texas Utilities Company (TXU Corp.)
- Michael McGreevy, SBC Communications Inc.
- Priscilla Myers, Prudential Insurance Company
- Stephen Perks, Gallaher Group plc
- Charmian Steven, Orange
- Robert Thurley, National Australia Bank Ltd.

PricewaterhouseCoopers Contributors:

This report also represents the efforts, knowledge and experience of many PricewaterhouseCoopers people from around the world:

Elizabeth A. Alexander	Ian J. Hollows
Harvey J. Bazaar	Ruud Kok
John P. Brolly	David L. McLean
Myra D. Cleary	Adil Nariman
John W. Copley	Judith Nicholl
Eric Dugelay	Bernadette Nye
Kenneth E. Dakdduk	Lawrence A. Ponemon
Daniel Fesson	Robert Rudloff
James S. Gerson	James F. Spitler
Laurent Gravier	Derek Trendell
Robert H. Herz	

We also gratefully acknowledge the contributions of former PricewaterhouseCoopers colleagues, Robert L. Gorvett, who as the initial project partner developed the research plan, and Jeffrey K. Rader, who served as a member of the core project team.

Additionally, we gratefully acknowledge support provided by William J. Duane, Jr., former General Auditor, Chemical Banking Corporation, in conducting many of the internal audit director interviews.

APPENDIX E
SELECTED BIBLIOGRAPHY

The following is a selection of key sources, including books, reports, articles and PricewaterhouseCoopers publications from which we drew:

The American Law Institute, Principles of Corporate Governance: Analysis and Recommendations, 1994

American Society of Corporate Secretaries, *Results of Survey on Audit Committee Effectiveness*, November 1998, via web site

Committee on Corporate Governance — Final Report, January 1998

Committee of Sponsoring Organizations of the Treadway Commission, *Fraudulent Financial Reporting 1987–1997*, March 1999

Committee of Sponsoring Organizations of the Treadway Commission, *Internal Control — Integrated Framework*, 1992

Corporate Governance — A Guide for Investment Managers and Corporations, Second Edition, Australian Investment Managers' Association, July 1997

National Association of Corporate Directors and The Center for Board Leadership, *Report of the NACD Blue Ribbon Commission on Audit Committees — A Practical Guide*, 2000

National Association of Corporate Directors, *1999–2000 Public Company Governance Survey*, October 1999

New York Stock Exchange and National Association of Securities Dealers, *Report and Recommendations of the Blue Ribbon Committee on Improving the Effectiveness of Corporate Audit Committees*, 1999

PricewaterhouseCoopers, *Audit Committees: Best Practices for Protecting Shareholder Interests*, 1999

PricewaterhouseCoopers, *Audit Committee Update 2000*, 2000

Public Oversight Board, *Final Report of the POB Panel on Audit Effectiveness*, 2000

IIA Research Foundation
Board of Research Advisors
2000/2001

♟ YES!

I would like to help The Foundation further the profession of internal auditing worldwide.

☐ I have enclosed a check made payable to The IIA Research Foundation in the amount of U.S. $_____

☐ I would like to make a gift by credit card in the amount of U.S. $_____
    ☐ VISA   ☐ MasterCard   ☐ American Express
    Card Number: _____ Exp. Date: _____ Signature:_____

☐ Please accept my pledge in the amount of U.S. $ _____, payable in the month of_____ ,
in the year _____.

(Please print the following information)

Name: _____ Title: _____

Organization: _____

Organization Address: _____

City: _____ State/Province: _____

Zip/Mail Code: _____ Country:_____

Tel: _____ Fax: _____ E-mail: _____

RETURN TO:
ĪIA The Institute of Internal Auditors Research Foundation
Attention: Eugene O'Neill
249 Maitland Avenue • Altamonte Springs, Florida • 32701-4201
Tel: +1-407-830-7600, Ext. 222 • Fax: +1-407-831-5171

ORDER FORM

Note: All orders must be prepaid. Use or copy this order form. To ensure immediate handling, please provide all information requested. Indicate "confirming copy" on any second requests of e-mail, fax, or telephone orders.

☐ **Charge to** (check one): ☐ VISA ☐ MasterCard ☐ American Express
Card #: _____ Expiration Date: _____ Signature: _____
☐ **Check Enclosed.** Make checks payable in U.S. funds to The Institute of Internal Auditors.
Ship to:
☐ IIA Member #: _____ ☐ Nonmember_____
Name:_____ Title: _____
Organization: _____ Organization Address: _____
City: _____ State/Province: _____
ZIP/Mail Code: _____ Country: _____ Phone: _____
Fax: _____ E-mail: _____
Special shipping instructions or remarks: _____
Please notify us if you have any special visual or audio requirements.

Title	Order No.	Qty.	Price	Total
Audit Committee Effectiveness – What Works Best	410		IIA Members $50; Nonmembers $65	
Corporate Governance and the Board – What Works Best	408		IIA Members $50; Nonmembers $65	
Package price for both	247		IIA Members $70; Nonmembers $100	

U.S. Federal Identification #: 13-5532538
Canadian GST Registration #: R123011538
Wire Transfer: First Union Bank
Ashford/Dunwoody Branch –
Account #: 2052500733784
Routing #: 061000227

Subtotal	
Tax, if applicable (see chart).	
Shipping and handling (see chart).	
For next day delivery within the U.S., add $20.	
Paying by check drawn on bank outside U.S., add $30.	
Paying by wire transfer, add collection fee of $15.	
Total	

Tax and Shipping Charges

Tax Charges:
Shipments to Florida, add 6% state tax plus your county surtax.
Shipments to Georgia, add 7% state tax.
Shipments to Canada, add 7% GST or 15% HST if applicable.

Standard Shipping Charges:
Within the United States, add 10% of total sales (not to exceed $60).
In Canada, add 15% of total sales (not to exceed $60).
Outside North America, add 30% of total sales.
Note: The IIA is not responsible for customs or broker's fees.

Express Shipping:
Available in United States only: Add $20.
All orders will normally be shipped by UPS or UPS International.
All orders by government purchase order are shipped FOB Point of Shipment.

PRICES SUBJECT TO CHANGE WITHOUT NOTICE

Five Easy Ways to Order!

 Online:
The IIA's Web site offers an interactive order form for your convenience. www.theiia.org

E-mail: iiapubs@pbd.com

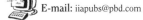 Mail:
IIA Distribution Center
C.S. 1616
Alpharetta, Georgia 30009-1616
U.S.A.

Fax: +1-770-442-9742

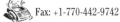 Telephone:
+1-877-867-4957 (toll free in U.S. and Canada) or
+1-770-442-8633, Ext. 275
Monday - Friday
8:00 a.m. – 5:30 p.m., EST